GROWING TOGETHER

THE COURSE

GROWING TOGETHER

THE COURSE

A complete marriage preparation programme

Andrew Body

CHURCH HOUSE PUBLISHING

Church House Publishing
Church House
Great Smith Street
London SW1P 3AZ

Tel: 020 7898 1451
Fax: 020 7898 1449

ISBN 978 0 7151 4135 9

Published 2007 by Church House Publishing.

The opinions expressed in this book are those of
the author and do not necessarily reflect the official
policy of the General Synod or The Archbishops'
Council of the Church of England.

Cover design by ie Design Consultancy

Printed in England by The Cromwell Press Ltd
Trowbridge, Wiltshire

Contents

Preface

Research is increasingly showing clearly that couples who take part in marriage preparation courses find it helpful. Over 90 per cent of the couples interviewed for the University of Surrey's 'Church Support of Marriage and Adult Relationships in Southern England' (2003) found it helpful and supportive. It is something they talk about warmly to their friends.

In addition, we need to be very positive in our encouragement for everyone who gets married in church to join in whatever we provide. The same research showed that couples wanted to feel that the church cared about their relationship. Offering good-quality marriage preparation is a very practical way of showing that care and commitment to them as people – and may well be the start of an ongoing relationship with the Church or the next step in a couple's faith journey.

Since the publication of my marriage preparation book *Growing Together*, I have been approached by a succession of people asking for help in how they might use the book for marriage preparation sessions with groups. It has been both gratifying and humbling to be told how useful and positive the book has proved. *Growing Together* was and is intended for couples to use on their own, and no course can possibly hope to cover all the ground the book does – unless people were to commit for a very large number of sessions. So what is offered here is a way in to some of the topics, in the hope that couples will then go on to explore the rest in their own time. I am not implying that the subjects included here are more important than the rest – but maybe they do provide a basis on which people can build.

What follow, after some preliminary practical issues, are three possible ways of using the *Growing Together* material:

- A Day Course of about five hours (including lunch)
- A Six plus One series of 90-minute sessions, which could be held weekly, fortnightly or monthly: the six sessions are about marriage and the one is about the wedding
- A Refresher Course for follow-up. In the form presented, this is designed for one 90-minute session, but it could easily be expanded. If run at the weekend, it might be combined with a lunch.

These are only suggestions. The six sessions could be delivered, with very little adaptation, as a two-day course, with the seventh session as a separate occasion at which other significant players in the drama can participate: organists, flower arrangers and so on.

Please use this material *your* way. What is provided is for you to adapt and shape for your particular circumstances. However you choose to use it, I hope you will find it beneficial as we seek to be alongside couples at this exciting time of their lives. May both you and those who attend have an enjoyable and productive time together.

Andrew Body

Practical matters

Numbers

In theory there are no limits to the numbers who might take part, other than the constraints imposed by the venue (see below). However, with less than three couples a course might feel threatening to people who are less articulate. There is also something to be said for having an equal number of couples, because then some activities can be done in fours.

If you don't have many weddings, there is a prior question about whether the group approach is the most appropriate. Or maybe this is an opportunity for co-operation with neighbouring parishes, or with ecumenical partners.

You will find full-colour invitations and a poster on the CD. Some churches make attendance more or less obligatory; others are less demanding. If we have a good product to offer people, we shouldn't be afraid to sell it. Language is important. Saying 'You have to attend' is off-putting; saying 'We assume that everyone will want to attend' is more friendly!

Venue

The numbers you expect will dictate the ideal size of the venue. Some church halls or village halls are admirably suited; others are not. But unless there is an exceptionally large house available, with many rooms that can be used, it probably has to be in a hall rather than a home. A few places have even hired hotel space – but that inevitably increases overheads considerably.

Key factors in deciding where to hold your course are:

- **Space**. Ideally you need a central meeting space and a number of side rooms, or other spaces where couples can talk with some degree of privacy.
- **Comfort**. A warm welcoming venue with comfortable, moveable chairs is important.
- **Kitchen facilities** are important, particularly for the day course.
- **Loos**, etc.

Arranging the space

Initially, the group should be placed in a circle, with the leader(s) placed at any point within that circle and not necessarily sitting together. Much of the work in these sessions is done by the individual couples on their own, so there needs to be space for them to be able to talk with some degree of privacy. Plenty of space is much more important than comfort.

If some couples are to be sent off to other rooms in the same building for their individual work, then you will need to think about how they are to know when to return. It may be important to have helpers who will alert them to finish that part of their discussion.

Costs

The courses assume that each couple will at some point receive a copy of *Growing Together*. Whether you are giving them the book as a gift from the church, or expecting them to buy it, or providing it within a charge for the whole course, including refreshments, is a matter for local decision. Unless you have to pay for hire of a venue, it ought to be possible to provide the book, a simple lunch at a day course, or coffee and biscuits at evening sessions, at a total charge of £10–£12. If you are also providing copies of the *Common Worship* Marriage Service booklet (which I would recommend) you will need to allow another £3 for that.

Equipment

Apart from copies of *Growing Together* and the Marriage Service, if you are providing that, you will need:

- A flip chart, or an overhead projector (OHP)
- Copies of the various questions and handouts, which are to be found in the Resource sheets of this book and on the CD-ROM. You will need to cut up the question sheets so that questions can be handed out individually.
- Drawing equipment and blank paper: either sheets from a flip chart or A4 sheets. (Flip chart paper is much the best for the exercise in Week Six of the longer course.)

Who can lead the course?

The course needs one or two people with group leadership skills to run it: not necessarily people who are specifically trained in marriage preparation, although that would be a great bonus when it is available. There is certainly no need for the leader to be the vicar! Depending on the format of your session(s), you will need to involve the clergy when the couples address questions about the service.

Nor is it necessary for the sessions to be run by a married couple. Indeed, there is some research that suggests this can be counterproductive, especially if the couple project their own relationship onto the participants. The participants are the experts on their own relationships.

Leading the course

The function of the leader(s) is to enable couples to articulate their responses. The leader will have to introduce the various topics. Some people who haven't done a great deal in this area may find it helpful to look at the complete 'scripts', which are to be found as Resource sheets 21–23 and on the CD-ROM. But it is better, whenever possible, for leaders to develop their own scripts, or to rework the material provided in their own way, and so to be more responsive to the way the group is developing. In the longer version I have suggested retelling some of the anecdotes in *Growing Together*, if leaders find them helpful. But don't use too many, or there will be no surprises when the participants read the book! In the end, whether every element suggested has been covered does not matter, because the couples will be able to do more when they work with the book on their own. You are simply setting them a pattern of how they can talk together about any issue. So if a particular part is arousing great interest, it might sometimes be right to give that an extra few minutes and omit something else.

The timings are given for guidance, not as a rigid plan. One of the roles the leaders must undertake is to be timekeepers of whatever version of the timetable they decide on. It is important to try to stick to the advertised length of the sessions, particularly for evening sessions, which often take place on weekday evenings.

The leader's role is not to listen in on the private discussions couples are having. Nor is the leader there to make any judgements about the couples. We are providing a space for couples to do some honest exploring for themselves.

Involving others

As well as those leading the sessions, other church members may be able to play a useful part by setting up the room, providing the refreshments and so on. But it is not a good idea to have too many non-participants floating around, in order to keep the focus on the work the couples themselves will do. Non-participants can be distracting, or seen as other 'experts' to whom reference can be made. We need to keep reminding ourselves that the purpose is for couples to learn *from each other*.

The Group Contract

It is good practice to have the group agree at the outset that what is said in the open forum of the group is to remain confidential to those who were present. It is also important that everyone is clear that at no point will they be under any pressure to say anything. If opinions or facts are being sought around the circle, then everyone has the right to say 'Pass'. We want people to feel safe in an environment that is probably entirely new to them. It would also be helpful to say, in the manner of the offers after some TV and radio programmes, that if any of the participants have been affected by any of the issues raised, then the leader will be happy to try to give suitable support, or direct them to where it can be found.

With so many personal issues at stake, it is very possible that some couples may find that the sessions raise topics they need to talk about individually. Offer to be a channel: you may not feel qualified to cope with some of the things they raise, but you can help them find someone who is.

The leader should undertake to start and finish the sessions at the times agreed, and those attending ongoing sessions should undertake to let the leader know if they will be missing or late, so that time will not be wasted for the other participants.

When to give out the copies of *Growing Together*

On a day course, or the longer course being run as a two-day event, I would suggest that the book is not given out until the end, although you will want to make reference to it earlier on.

On the seven-week course, you will have to decide what suits your group best. If it is being run weekly, there is still an argument for leaving it to the end. If couples work on the appropriate chapters immediately, there will be less left for them to do in the remaining weeks and months before the wedding. On the other hand, if you are having monthly sessions, then it is probably best to give the book out at the end of the first week, with guidance about which chapters they can look at in order to follow up what has been done that evening. Asking them not to look at the rest of the book may be looking for a level of restraint that most people do not have – but nonetheless is worth saying!

Prayers

Most groups will include both people with some faith and people with none. It is good to model the practice of simple, straightforward and relevant prayer, but important not to put off those who are on the very fringes of the church. Ending a session with an opportunity to be quiet and reflect for a minute or so on the points that have been raised, then ending the reflection time with a short prayer, is less daunting to such people than beginning the sessions with prayer. The following is offered as a model, not a script! You might find other suitable prayers in *Pocket Prayers for Marriage* (also published by Church House Publishing), which my wife and I compiled.

> ***Loving God, we thank you for the things which have been in our minds. Help us to go on growing together in understanding and love for each other. Amen.***

How to use this material

This book (and the supporting CD-ROM), together with *Growing Together* and the *Common Worship* Marriage Service, provide all the material you need to run the course. Each session contains a mix of input by the leader and exercises to be done in pairs or groups. After some exercises there will be an opportunity for feedback in a whole group (although do stress that there is no obligation to share if people feel uncomfortable doing so). Others are for the couples only – and if that is the case, it is important to make it clear beforehand that no feedback is expected after those exercises.

The suggested talks cover the same range of themes as are covered in *Growing Together*.

Leaders have a number of options on how they choose to deliver the talks. In the session itself, the suggested content for the talk is outlined in a bullet list. For those who would prefer to have a full script to work from, these are provided at the back of the book and on the CD-ROM. In either case, leaders are encouraged to adapt the talks as they see fit and to deliver these in a style that suits them.

Make sure you are well prepared for each session – you will find a checklist at the start of each session. Leaders need to think through the following:

- Room layout and other working spaces (see above)
- How many other helpers are needed to keep things flowing smoothly
- How they will deliver the talks
- How the exercises will work (Are extra materials required? Are there worksheets to be downloaded or photocopied in advance?)
- Equipment required, e.g. a flip chart or OHP, pens and paper, CD-player.

Key to the icons

Both the day course and each session of the seven-week course contain a mixture of the following:

 Introduction to the day/evening session: An opportunity to welcome everyone, to outline what is going to happen in terms of timings, content and refreshment breaks and to reassure those who are a little nervous! Humour often helps here. Suggestions for anecdotes etc. are included in the supporting scripts.

 Input from the leader(s) introducing the exercises.

 Individual work: Individuals working by themselves.

 Couples' exercise: an exercise to be done in couples, with feedback of some kind to the whole group.

 Couples' exercise: an exercise to be done by couples, but without feedback.

 Group exercise or discussion

 Feedback: An opportunity for couples or the group as a whole to give feedback. Leaders may wish to write comments on a flip chart or OHP.

 Refreshment break

 Questions: An opportunity for group members to ask any questions that have arisen as a result of the session.

 Concluding reflection and/or prayer

Using the CD-ROM

Contents

- The resource sheets (including the full scripts)
- Audio files (see below)
- Course Invitations
- Course Poster
- Illustrations from *Growing Together*
- Extracts from the prefaces to the marriage service from the *Common Worship* Marriage Service and the *Book of Common Prayer* Marriage Service

Running the CD-ROM

Windows PC users:

The CD-ROM should start automatically. If you need to start the application manually, click on the Start and select Run, then type d\growingtogether.exe (where d is the letter of your CD-ROM drive) and click on OK.

The menu that appears gives you access to all the resources on the CD. No software is installed on to your computer.

Mac users:

The CD-ROM should start automatically. If you need to start the application manually, click on the CD icon on your desktop.

Viruses

We have checked the CD-ROM for viruses throughout its creation. However, you are advised to run your own virus-checking software over the CD-ROM before using it. Church House Publishing and The Archbishops' Council accept no responsibility for damage or loss of data on your systems, however caused.

Copyright

The scripts and resource sheets are copyright © Andrew Body 2007. All other material on the CD-ROM is copyright © The Archbishops' Council 2007, unless otherwise specified. All industry trademarks are acknowledged. You are free to use this material within your own church or group, but the material must not be further distributed in any form without written permission from The Copyright Administrator (copyright@c-of-e.org.uk). When using the resources from the CD-ROM please include the appropriate copyright notice.

Audio

The CD contains audio files which can be played in an ordinary CD player or on a computer. They are:

- Track 1: An interview with Andrew Body about *Growing Together* and marriage preparation.

- Tracks 2–8: A short introduction to each week for the minister or course leader. These tracks are NOT designed to be played during the course.
- Track 9: Closing reflections and prayer. This track has been recorded with those being prepared for marriage in mind, and can be played at or near the end of the course.

Resources

The written resources require Adobe Acrobat Reader (Preview for Mac users) for display and printing. If Acrobat Reader is already installed on your computer, it will be loaded automatically whenever required. If you do not have it, you can install Acrobat Reader by downloading the reader from www.adobe.com.

Error Messages

You may receive the error message, 'There is no application associated with the given file name extension'. If you are trying to read one of the pdf files, you should install the Adobe Acrobat Reader and try again.

Links

The links to the web sites require an active Internet connection. Please ensure you can browse the Web before selecting an external web site.

A one-day course

Questions for couples are found in Resource sheet 1 and on the CD-ROM.

A scripted version (for those who prefer it) can be found at Resource sheet 21 and on the CD-ROM.

Suggested timetable for the day

9.30 a.m.	Arrivals and coffee
10.00 a.m.	**Introduction** (10–15 minutes)
10.15 a.m.	**Why this one?** (Exercise: 20 minutes)
10.35 a.m.	**Interactive talk: Past, present and future** (45 minutes, in 3 × 15-minute slots)
11.20 a.m.	**Coffee break** (15 minutes)
11.35 a.m.	**Interactive talk: Five topics (Sex, Children, Companionship, Communication, Conflict)** (70 minutes)
12.45 a.m.	**Pre-lunch summing-up and time for questions**
1.00 p.m.	**Lunch break** (45 minutes)
1.45 p.m.	**Faith** (15–20 minutes)
2.05 p.m.	**Making decisions about the wedding** (55 minutes)
3.00 p.m.	**Summing-up, final questions and farewells** (15 minutes).

Preparation checklist

- A warm room, with enough chairs – preferably comfortable ones – for every participant
- If possible, other spaces to which couples can spread for their private discussions
- Photocopies of the questions, cut so that each question can be handed out separately: there should be one copy for each *person*, not one for each couple
- Photocopies of any worksheets: again, there should be one for each *person*, not one for each couple
- Pens
- Paper
- Flip chart or OHP
- CD-player
- Refreshments.

Timings

All the timings provided are for guidance only. How long it takes people to move to the places where they work as couples or smaller groups, and how fast you speak when doing your input, will affect how long you have to work with. The important thing is to keep to time, as far as you can, for *each section as a whole*, and not to worry too much about the timings within each section. If in doubt, say less yourself and let them talk more!

Introduction

(10–15 minutes – will depend on the number of participants)

- The leader welcomes couples to the day and outlines the order of events. This is an opportunity to set people at their ease. Humour often lightens the mood; see the script for suitable anecdotes.
- Make sure that couples are aware of matters of confidentiality. Outline the way the day will run: make couples aware of the group and couples' exercises, but make sure that everyone is aware that no one is under any obligation to share if they prefer not to.
- Explain that doing something like this is a worthwhile investment of time. Unless people have an opportunity to stand back and think about what they are doing, they can find that their energies are easily diverted onto secondary issues and not the relationship itself. The way we will be working some of the time – giving each other one-to-one space to talk and think – is a model for how they can interact throughout their lives together.
- Establish the Group Contract, underlining the following:
    - Confidentiality
    - Mostly talking privately in pairs, but *no obligation* to share anything
    - When we work together, everyone has the right to say 'Pass'
    - Timekeeping
    - Living with frustration – they will want to have had more time on some things, but there is a lot to get through – they can always go on talking at home!

Introductions

Go round the group and invite each couple to:

- give their names
- tell the group:
    - How long they have known each other
    - How long they have been living together (if they have)
    - When they are getting married
- Leader(s) should also introduce themselves, using the same format as far as possible. If a leader goes first, it will model how you hope others will respond and give the first couple a little time to get their thoughts together.

How are you feeling?

- Still as a whole group, ask each person to share one word giving their feelings about this course. Explain that if someone else uses their word before they do, they don't need to think of another, but can just repeat it. It will be interesting to see what feelings are shared.
- List the words on flip chart or OHP.
- Leaders may then give a brief comment on the range and/or commonality of the feelings expressed.

Why this one?

(20 minutes)

If numbers allow, ask each couple to join with another couple. If not, this can be done in pairs. The timings will depend on which option you choose. If they are working in pairs, you will have more time for group feedback.

In the fours, or pairs, encourage each person to spend a couple of minutes saying why, out of all humanity, they have chosen their partner as the one to marry. Encourage them to focus on what is it about him or her that makes them want to do that. Invite them to see how much they can embarrass each other!

Do make it clear that there will be no detailed reporting back from this session, so they only have to say something in front of two other people who are in the same boat.

Did couples find their reasons were the same? Similar? Or quite different?

Explain that that is why no one can advise anyone else on how to be married. We all have different needs, expectations and fears. Many will have watched *The Good Life*. Tom and Barbara are happily married, and so are Margot and Gerry; but none of them could possibly be married to their 'opposite number' in the other house.

If they don't know that programme, suggest they think of their favourite soap, and why each of the pairs of partners in those stories is different from all the other pairs. They are already involved in an adventure of getting to know another person better than anyone else in the world – and maybe discovering things about themselves as well.

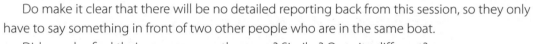

Past, present and future

(45 minutes – in 3 × 15-minute segments)

The past

Introduction (5 minutes)

Explain that for the next 45 minutes you will be helping the group to explore three vital times: the past, the present and the future. It would seem logical to start with the past.

Start with another exercise. Go around the group and ask everyone to share something about themselves that their partner (as far as they are aware) doesn't know. It may be something that happened to them when they were very small, or it may be something that happened yesterday. It need not be anything very important – even what they had for lunch, if they can't think of anything else!

- Draw out the fact that we can't know everything about each other; the couples won't have had time to share everything that has happened to each partner, and some things surface from memory only when an event triggers them.
- Remind them that some memories have been buried because they are painful. The intimacy of a marriage is sometimes the first place where such memories can be faced.
- Our images of marriage are formed by the homes in which we grew up. Point out that within the group there may be people who have experienced more than one

marriage of their parents, or who have been brought up by a single parent. For those who have not seen a marriage working 'from the inside', memories may be replaced by fantasies of what a marriage 'ought' to be like.

- Ask the couples to spend about ten minutes sharing with each other good and bad things that come from their experience in the past. What are the things about the marriages they have been part of as children that they would want to be the same in their own marriage? What things would they want to be different? They might like to think about whether those things are the same as their partner's, or different. There is no reporting back after this exercise – this is their private discussion.

Hand out the first question from Resource sheet 1.

The future

Introduction and drawing (5 minutes)

Explain that although they started, logically, with the past, they will now go on, illogically, to the future. The marriage industry thrives on dreams. There is an old joke about the dreams that brides have about their wedding day. They dream about walking down the aisle to the altar and singing a hymn. So they have those three words in their mind: I'll – alter – him!

Ask the participants, first of all as individuals, to draw something that represents what they dream their married life will be like in, say, ten years' time. Suggest they might want to draw a real picture, or maybe symbols – like £ signs to indicate that by then they expect to have made their fortune. Emphasize that only their partner will see their 'work of art'. Give them two or three minutes to draw something individually which is 'Us in ten years' time'.

(There is a sheet for this at Resource sheet 2 and on the CD-ROM.)

Then ask each participant to go off with their partner and talk about their pictures for five minutes. Ask them, if they are willing, when the group comes back together, to share whether their dreams are exactly the same.

When the couples come back together, ask them to share whether their dreams turned out to be largely the same, or not. How does that make people feel?

The present

Introduction (7 minutes)

Explain that the reason we are coming to the present last of all is because there is a sense in which the present is the melting pot in which their history and their dreams meet. Every day they are using the past and the future to create this moment.

Ask them to share briefly with everyone what it feels like to be at this stage, when the wedding is booked and the plans are being made. What are the best and worst things about this stage for them as a couple?

Prepare the couples now to do some private sharing about what difference getting married is going to make. If they are not yet living together, there will be some pretty basic changes, but it is worth spelling these out. But if they are already together, in a sense this question is even more important. Do they expect getting married to make a difference, or not? If so, what difference will it make? If not, why not? Point out that if they say 'No', then it will be worth exploring why they do actually want to get married. If they say 'Yes', then what does that say about the development of their relationship, and how it might move on? Remind them that on this occasion there is no reporting back. Someone will come to tell them that time is up, and coffee is ready.

Hand out the second question from Resource sheet 1.

Coffee break

Five topics

(70 minutes)

Introduction (3 minutes)

- Explain that between now and lunch, five topics will be opened up that are pretty important. The first three are reasons given in the wedding service for getting married, and the other two are things that underlie lots of other topics they might want to talk about in detail at another time. Say you will be explaining how they might do that just before lunch.
- Read the reasons as they come in *Common Worship*. They are the same in the other orders of service that are still legal, although in a different order. The order is not particularly important. As well as being printed here, these reasons can be found on the CD-ROM.

> *The gift of marriage brings husband and wife together*
> *in the delight and tenderness of sexual union*
> *and joyful commitment to the end of their lives.*
> *It is given as the foundation of family life*
> *in which children are [born and] nurtured*
> *and in which each member of the family,*
> *in good times and in bad,*
> *may find strength, companionship and comfort,*
> *and grow to maturity in love.*

Sex

(12 minutes)

Introduction (5 minutes)

We take the reasons in the order in which they come. Sex is the first – and the service is daring enough to use the word 'sexual'. Cover the following points:

- Sex is God's gift to us and, far from being naughty, it is something holy and wonderful and to be celebrated. But like any other skill, although it is the most natural thing in the world, it has to be learned, and their task is to be each other's teacher.

- However good their sex education may have been, they need to go on learning from each other, both now and in the future.
- Raise the question of what attitudes to sex were in their upbringing. Did their parental homes have the same attitudes to sex, and to nudity, for example?
- Reassure them that many couples take time to settle down sexually. That is normal; but if problems persist, it is good to seek help earlier rather than later.

Sex is intimate and private, so now ask them to go with their own partner again and just share a little about one question. Assure them they will not be asked to report back on this one! 'What does sex add to your whole relationship?'

Hand out the third question from Resource sheet 1.

Children
(15 minutes)

Introduction (5 minutes)

Ask whether they put any children in their 'dream' pictures of what they expect in ten years' time (including any either of them may already have). Then cover the following points:

- Changing family sizes, for economic reasons
- Changing age at which people begin families
- Changing 'shape' of marriages: longer life and better contraception mean that more time is spent as a couple before and after child-rearing
- Increasing worries about fertility (one couple in six go to the doctor – happily, most of these couples do not have a serious problem and find that they can eventually conceive)
- More choices about medical intervention if there is a problem (IVF, etc.)
- One or both partners may already have children.

Ask them, as couples again, to take ten minutes to talk about how they would feel if they had difficulty conceiving, and what they would want to do. Explain that if they are a couple who don't want to have children (or to have any more children), they might like instead to talk about what they would do if they found they *had* conceived. Tell them that, again, there will no reporting back.

Hand out the fourth question from Resource sheet 1.

Companionship
(15 minutes)

Introduction (5 minutes)

The third reason in the service is companionship, or friendship. Include the following points:

- Most couples meet as friends first of all, before they fall in love. For some, that means that friendship gets pushed into second place – being lovers is the task of the moment. But at the end of the day, friendship is the longest lasting of all these three.
- Sex will still be important when they are 80, but it will be less important than now.

- If they have children, these will hopefully have left home by then. But they themselves might be leaning on each other literally as well as metaphorically. Being friends is a basic requirement for a good marriage.
- Many people include in their wedding service those famous words from Kahlil Gibran's *The Prophet*:

> *And stand together, yet not too near together,*
> *For the pillars of the temple stand apart*
> *And the oak tree and the cypress grow not in each other's shadow.*

- How we spend time – together and apart, with friends as well as with each other – is something we all have to negotiate.

Ask each individual to talk to someone other than their partner for a minute or two about this sort of thing, and how they handle togetherness and apartness in their relationship.

Discussion with someone else **(2 minutes)**

General discussion **(8 minutes)**

Communication
(15 minutes)

Introduction (2 minutes)

Include the following:

- Good communication is a basic skill. Certainly the most common thing people say when they go for marriage counselling is that communications have broken down.
- There are two elements. The first is talking – because if people do not talk to each other, how can they know what the other one thinks and feels?
- The second skill is listening. If people do not listen, it doesn't matter how much someone talks.
- Explain that for the exercises they will do now they will all stay in the main meeting-room, although they will be working in pairs. Before they do some talking and listening in a moment – and to remind them that words are not the only way of communicating – ask them first to hold their intended's hand, and to take it in turn to express an emotion by the way in which they hold it. Ask them to close their eyes, or else they will also be using facial expressions, which is another important way of communicating.

Hand messages **(2 minutes)**

- Explain we will now try some ways of listening and talking.
- Ask each person to find someone other than their partner and to talk to them for a minute, non-stop, about what they did yesterday. Explain that both of them must do this *at the same time* – just talk *at* each other without listening to the other. It's up to both of them to keep going.

Simultaneous talk **(1 minute)**

In the full group, ask how that felt. **(2 minutes)**

Now ask each person to work with their proper partner. Ask one person in each couple first of all to tell a story for two minutes – perhaps about something that happened to them when the other person wasn't there. Ask the other person to do their very best to ignore their partner. Suggest they look the other way; fiddle with their watch; whatever they like – but don't pay any attention.

Ignored talk (**2 minutes**)

In the full group, ask how that felt. (**2 minutes**)

Now ask them to reverse roles, so that the 'rude' one becomes the storyteller. They again have two minutes. But this time the listener should pay full attention. Tell the participants that this time there will be no feedback.

Careful listening (**2 minutes**)

Ask the 'listener' now to recount that story to the 'storyteller'. They have one minute. Ask them also to say what *emotions* were coming over to them. What did it feel like to be listened to? Were they heard accurately?

This time there will be no feedback.

Recall (**1 minute**)

All those things can and do happen in relationships. People talk at each other without listening. They ignore each other. And sometimes they listen with full attention: sometimes to the facts, and sometimes also to the emotions – to what is not being said in words. People can all improve their listening and talking skills. The Children's Society once ran a very perceptive campaign under the slogan 'This child needs a good listening to'.

Conflict
(15 minutes)

Introduction (**2 minutes**)

Hand out the worksheet with four rough graphs (*Resource sheet 3*).

Cover the following points:

- The first three are unrealistic maps of how a marriage will be. The first represents ever-increasing bliss. The second represents ever-increasing misery. The third represents no change at all – everything just as it is, for ever.
- Explain that if any of those is their picture of how their relationships will be, then they have a problem.
- The last one is the reality.
- There will be ups and downs in everyone's relationships. The vital thing is how they are handled.
- Ask them to have a go, individually, at plotting on the back of that sheet a graph of how they as individuals see their relationship so far. Hopefully there haven't been any major downs, but there will almost certainly have been little blips – maybe stresses caused from outside, when a house purchase fell through, or when there was a bereavement.

Individual graph plotting (3 minutes)

- Ask the participants then to go with their partner to compare notes and talk about what they have each drawn, and whether they have each seen the ups and downs in the same way.
- Then, lastly, ask them to think about the skills they have that help them to cope with the less good moments: the irritations and crossed wires that happen. How do they get through those? How do they make up? Suggest thinking of their own skills in terms of a first-aid box. What are the equivalent first-aid things that help bandage their relationships when they get bruised? Suggest things like being good at listening; giving each other space; having a sense of humour. Remind participants they have ten minutes for these two tasks – reflecting on their graphs and thinking about their first-aid box – and can divide the time as they prefer.
- Hand out the fifth and sixth questions from Resource sheet 1.

Sharing in pairs (10 minutes)

Pre-lunch summary

(up to 15 minutes)

Introduction (3 minutes)

Cover the following:

- They have picked up five topics, and really only scratched the surface of those. They could have spent all morning on just one.
- They could equally well have talked about how they get on with the wider family; how they see their roles; how they cope with money – the list is endless.
- At the end of this day they are going to get a copy of a book called *Growing Together*, which was written by a clergyman with a great deal of experience of working with couples, not only in his parish but as a marriage counsellor. The book is designed for couples to use on their own, to help them deepen their understanding of each other. They have used this morning about 8 of the 150 questions in the book. It also has some stories of real people, who might provoke some discussion as well. Each chapter is structured around those three topics they started with: past, present and future.
- Explain that after lunch they will pick up one other topic from the book, and also look at some practical issues about the wedding day itself, rather than the state of being married. If there is time, offer an opportunity for general reaction and questions to the day so far.

Questions and comments (Up to 12 minutes, unless there has been time slippage earlier!)

Lunch break **(45 minutes)**

Faith

(15–20 minutes)

 Introduction (2 minutes)

- The fact that they have decided to get married in church was bound to open up questions of faith. Point out that among the group there are probably both people who are regular worshippers and people who have never set foot in the church. Somehow or other, all of them have come to the decision that a church wedding is what they want.
- Ask them each to write on a piece of paper *their own* reason for getting married in church: not their reason as a couple; not their partner's reason; but *their own*. Ask them to be ruthlessly honest: if the reason is to keep their parents quiet, or whatever, then they should say so! Assure them that you will mix up all the pieces of paper before reading them out.

 Individual work **(2 minutes)**

Sharing (on flip chart or OHP if desired) **(5 minutes)**

 Talk **(1–3 minutes)**

Cover the following points:

- Everyone is on a faith journey of some kind.
- We are all believers or non-believers: we all have a religious 'position' *now*.
- Those positions may change during the time they are married. That will affect both of them.
- There will be other faith decisions to make: for example, whether any children will be baptized.

Sometimes people think it is strange that people who don't usually go to church want to have their wedding there. Ask them to imagine they are being interviewed for a TV programme by someone who thinks like that. What are the things they would want to say in reply. No reporting back – their private discussion for eight minutes.

Hand out the seventh question from Resource sheet 1.

 Sharing in pairs **(8 minutes)**

Making decisions about the wedding

(50 minutes)

 It is their day – and the choices are theirs. So they should personalize as much as they can. They may want to involve other people in what happens. They do need, however, to check with the vicar everything they would like to do.

Resource sheet 17 is a worksheet that can be used as it is or adapted to suit local usage. The sections and lists below provide you with an aide-memoire of the areas that need to be considered. Some of them will be irrelevant in your situation, but there may be others you need to add.

Order of service

Strictly speaking, there are three orders of service that are legal: the 1662 Book of Common Prayer, the 1928 Prayer Book (Series 1) and *Common Worship* (2000). In practice *Common Worship* probably has everything participants might want, including a form of marriage service with Holy Communion, which is an option any couples who are regular communicants might like to consider. It doesn't necessarily add a lot of time to the service.

Choreography

Explain that couples will need to decide . . .

- Who walks in with whom
- When (and where) people should stand or sit
- On 'giving away' or alternatives
- Where the registers are signed
- Other practical issues

Hymns

Explain that . . .

- There is space in the service for four, but they don't have to have that many.
- The most important thing is that people know the hymns chosen. It's embarrassing for everyone if the vicar has to sing a solo!
- Some hymns fit in one place better than another. So, for example, a hymn about vows goes well at the point when they are about to make theirs; or a hymn which is a prayer just before the prayers. It's also generally best to go out on the most joyous note.
- It's also important for them to check that the tune the organist has in mind is also the tune they are expecting. Some popular hymns, such as 'Love divine' or 'At the name of Jesus', have more than one well-known tune.
- Copyright issues need to be checked.
- It's a good idea to start thinking now! People often pick up ideas when they go to church on Sundays, or to other people's weddings.
- Not all churches have organists who can play anything that is put in front of them. Discussion with the clergy is important, in case there are any local restrictions to bear in mind.

Readings

- Who? This is a good opportunity to involve other people, but do stress the need for readers to practise, particularly if there are tricky names in the readings chosen.

- What? At least one of the readings must be from the Bible. There are 26 suggestions in *Common Worship* (but they can choose others if they wish).

- Take care to read all the suggested Bible readings, and then cut them down to a short list. Why do these particular readings speak to them?

- Share with the group one or two of the less well-known readings: for example, the one from the Song of Solomon (sometimes called 'the Song of Songs'). Explain it is a really quite erotic poem that talks about God's love in terms of human passion. The reading doesn't include the parts about the beloved's breasts being like twin fawns, or clusters of grapes, or the man's legs being like alabaster columns set upon bases of gold. This is the bit that it does use: they need to think of a woman hiding behind the lattice window of a Middle Eastern house, with the lover whispering through the window. (Incidentally, it says in another place that he has arrived there bounding like a young gazelle across the desert!) This is how it goes . . .

- Read the Song of Solomon passage (the text is on Resource sheet 19 and also on the CD-ROM).

- The second is from the Apocrypha – the books from Old Testament times that were left out of some versions of the Bible. This one is from the book of Tobit.

- Read the Tobit passage (the text is on Resource sheet 19 and also on the CD-ROM).

- Explain that the context of that one is rather fun. The couple are praying before their first night together. But Sarah has been previously given in marriage to seven other men. Unfortunately, before the marriage was consummated they were all killed by a demon called Asmodeus. Now, people were as sceptical about the reality of demons then as they are today, and they quite reasonably said it was Sarah who had killed off the men. Tobias is very smitten with Sarah, but he has a meeting with the Archangel Raphael and, after another curious incident when a huge fish tries to swallow Tobias's foot when he washes it in the Tigris, he is told by the angel to catch the fish and eat its flesh, but to keep the gall, heart and liver, because they are useful in dealing with demons. So, come his first night with Sarah, when they are obviously both on edge that he might become Victim Number Eight, he takes the precaution of burning these bits of old fish guts as a way of dealing with Asmodeus – which works. Apparently it smells so bad he takes off to Upper Egypt, where Raphael deals with him once and for all.

- Make sure the reader has the right translation – and knows which one will be on the lectern at the service.

- Non-biblical readings are very personal and entirely optional. The most important thing is that what is chosen means something to the couple. All of these need to be OK'd with the vicar. Some brave brides and grooms have written something themselves.

Prayers

- Yet again, a time when couples can make the service very much their own.
- One set of prayers is printed in the main text, but there are many others in *Common Worship: Pastoral Services*. The Marriage Service does not reprint all the alternatives. The idea generally is that they choose one of the longer ones (with the 'response' style) or one from each of the sections of short ones.
- Prayers from elsewhere can also be used.
- Or couples can write their own.

Music

Music sets the tone and is an important part of the service.

- There are three basic places to have music:
  - Entry
  - Registers – probably 5–7 minutes' worth
  - Exit.
- Organ music is normal – but do make sure that the pieces of music will suit both the building and the organ. People are sometimes led astray by listening to discs. It's also important to check that the organist can play the pieces chosen!
- Recordings may perhaps be used, if a system to play them is available.
- Is live music from friends or family an option?

Oddments

- Banns
- Fees
- Confetti
- Photos and/or videos
- Other practical issues

Ending

(10 minutes)

- Thank them for coming.
- Invite final questions.
- Say that if personal issues which are causing them concern have been raised during the sessions, anyone affected should speak to the leader afterwards.
- Give out books.
- Use the prayer below to end.

There are so many choices:
    venues and menus,
    dresses and tresses,
    shades and bridesmaids,
    cars and guitars,
    houses and blouses,
    speeches and preachers;
It is so easy to over-spend, to lose all sense of proportion.
Help us to plan not only for the day, but for the rest of our life.
Help us to choose the best things:
    faith
    hope
    love.

(Andrew Body, from *Pocket Prayers for Marriage*)

There is an audio file on the CD-ROM of Andrew reading a concluding prayer, which you may wish to use at the end of this session.

A six- plus one-week course

Questions for the participants will be found in Resource sheets 5, 6, 9, 10 and 13 and on the CD-ROM.

A scripted version, for those who prefer it, can be found at Resource sheet 22 and on the CD-ROM.

Preparation checklist

- A warm room with enough chairs – preferably comfortable ones – for every participant.
- If possible, other spaces to which couples can spread for their private discussions.
- Photocopies of the questions in Resource sheets 5, 6, 9, 10 and 13 appropriate to each session, cut so that each question can be handed out separately. There should be one copy for each *person*, not one for each couple.
- Photocopies of any worksheets. There should be one copy for each *person*, not one for each couple.
- Pens
- Paper
- Flip chart or OHP
- CD-player
- Refreshments.

Timings

All the timings provided are for guidance only. How long it takes people to move to the places where they work as couples or smaller groups, and how fast you speak when doing your input, will affect how long you have to work with. The important thing is to keep to time, as far as you can, for *each section as a whole*, and not worry too much about the timings within each section. If in doubt, say less and let them talk more!

Week 1

Introductions; past, present and future

Introduction

(20 minutes – will depend on the number of participants)

- Welcome the couples to the course. This is an opportunity to set people at their ease. Humour often breaks the ice. See the script (*Resource sheet 22*) for suitable anecdotes.

- Make sure that couples are aware of matters of confidentiality. Outline the way the course will run: make couples aware of the group and couples' exercises, but make sure that everyone is aware that no one is under any obligation to share if they prefer not to.

- Explain that doing something like this is a worthwhile investment of time. Unless people have an opportunity to stand back and think about what they are doing, they can find their energies are easily diverted onto secondary issues, rather than the relationship itself. The way we will be working some of the time – giving each other one-to-one space to talk and think – is a model for how they can interact throughout their lives together.

- Establish the Group Contract, underlining the following:
    - Confidentiality
    - Mostly talking privately in pairs, but with *no obligation* to share anything
    - When we work together, everyone has the right to say 'Pass'
    - Timekeeping
    - Living with frustration: they will want to have had more time on some things, but there is a lot to get through – they can always go on talking at home!

Introductions

Go round the group and invite each couple to:

- give their names
- tell the group:
    - How long they have known each other
    - How long they have been living together (if they have)
    - When they are getting married.

- You should also introduce yourself, using the same format as far as possible. If a leader goes first, it will model how you hope others will respond and also give the first couple a little time to get their thoughts together.

- Still as a whole group, ask each person to share one word about their feelings about this course. Explain that if someone else uses their word first, they don't need to think of another but just repeat it. It will be interesting to see what feelings are shared.

- List the words used on a flip chart or OHP.
- You may then give a brief comment on the range and/or commonality of feelings.

Introduce the course as a whole:

- Some of the topics which will be covered
- Practical arrangements
- Mention the book to be given, either on this occasion and/or at the end of the course.

Past, present and future

(70 minutes)

The past

(15 minutes)

Introduction (5 minutes)

Explain that for the rest of the evening they will be exploring three vital times – the past, the present and the future. Logically, they will start with the past.

Start with an exercise. Go around the group and ask everyone to share something that their partner (as far as they are aware) does not know. It may be something that happened to them when they were very small, or it may be something that happened yesterday. It doesn't have to be anything very important – even what they had for lunch, if they can't think of anything else!

- Draw out that we can't know everything about each other – they will not yet have had time to share everything that has happened to them, and some things surface from memory only when an event triggers it.
- Remind them that some memories are buried because they are painful. The intimacy of a marriage is sometimes the first place where these can be faced.
- Tell the story of Paula and Graham (*Growing Together*, p. 16).
- Our images of marriage are formed by the homes in which we grew up. Point out that within the group there may be people who have experienced more than one marriage of their parents, or who have been brought up by a single parent. For those who have not seen a marriage working 'from the inside', memories may be replaced by fantasies of what a marriage 'ought' to be like.

- Ask the couples to spend about ten minutes sharing with each other good and bad things that come from their experience in the past. What are the things about the marriages they have been part of as children that they want to keep in their own marriage? What things would they want to be different? They might like to think about whether those things are the same as their partners, or different. There is no reporting back after this exercise – this is their private discussion.

Hand out the first question (*Resource sheet 5*).

The future
(25 minutes)

Introduction (5 minutes)

- Explain that although they started, logically, with the past, they will now go on, illogically, to the future. The marriage industry thrives on dreams. There is an old joke about the dreams that brides have about their wedding day. They dream about walking down the aisle to the altar and singing a hymn. So they have those three words in their minds: 'I'll – alter – him!'

- First of all, ask the participants as individuals, to draw something that represents what they dream their married life will be like in, say, ten years' time. Suggest they might want to draw a real picture, or maybe symbols – like £ signs to indicate that they expect to have made their fortunes! Emphasize that only their partner will see their 'work of art'. Give them two or three minutes to draw something individually that is 'Us in ten years' time'. (*There is a sheet for this at Resource sheet 2 and on the CD-ROM.*)

Then ask them to go off with their partner and each talk about their pictures for five minutes. Ask them if they are willing, when the group comes back together, to share whether their dreams turned out to be exactly the same.

Hand out Question 2 from Resource sheet 5.

Ask them to share whether their dreams were largely the same. How does that make people feel?

The present
(20 minutes)

Introduction (10 minutes)

- Explain that the reason we are coming to the present last of all is because there is a sense in which the present is the melting pot in which their history and their dreams meet. Every day they are using the past and the future to create this moment.

- Ask them to share briefly with each other what it feels like to be at this stage, when the wedding is booked and the plans are being made. What are the best and worst things about this stage for them as a couple?

Sharing (on a flip chart or OHP if desired)

Prepare them now to do some private sharing about what differences getting married will make. If they are not living together, there will be some pretty basic changes, but it is worth spelling these out. But if they are already together, in a sense the question is even more important. Do they expect getting married to make a difference, or not? If so, what difference will it make? If not, why not? Point out that if they say 'No', then they may want to explain why they *do* want to get married. If they say 'Yes', then what is that saying about the development of their relationship and how it might move on? Remind them that on this occasion there is no reporting back. Someone will come to tell them that time is up.

Hand out Question 3 from Resource sheet 5.

If timings have gone well, there should now be about ten minutes left. If not, you will need to edit or omit all or part of this final section.

Ending

(10 minutes)

Hand out copies of Resource sheet 4.

Explain that on the piece of paper provided they will find two columns. One has an exclamation mark above it, the other a question mark.

Ask them each to jot down *individually* under the exclamation mark any new thought that has occurred to them this evening. It need not be anything profound! And under the question mark to put down anything that has raised questions they want to pursue further. Say that there will be an opportunity at the beginning of next week, if they want it, to share anything that has come out of this evening; but there will be no pressure to say anything, if they prefer not to.

Individual responses (2 minutes)

Ask them to share with someone *other* than their partner any 'exclamation mark' thoughts that have come to them as a result of this evening.

Sharing in pairs (2 minutes)

Then ask them to share with their *real* partner any 'question mark' areas that have come up this evening and which they would like to explore further with each other.

Sharing as couples (2 minutes)

Say that if personal issues have been raised during the session which are causing them concern, they should speak to the leader afterwards.

Lastly, ask them to take a minute or two in silence to reflect on all that has been said during the session, together and privately. Explain that you will then offer all those thoughts to God in a short prayer to close.

Week 2
Reasons for getting married

Preparation checklist

- A warm room with enough chairs – preferably comfortable ones – for every participant.
- If possible, other spaces to which couples can spread for their private discussions.
- Photocopies of the questions in Resource sheet 6, cut so that each question can be handed out separately. There should be one copy for each *person*, not one for each couple.
- Photocopies of any worksheets. There should be one for each *person*, not one for each couple.
- Pens
- Paper
- Flip chart or OHP
- CD-player
- Refreshments.

Introduction

(20 minutes)

Welcome them back. Express the hope that, if they had things they wanted to discuss further with each other, they have found time to do it.

Invite anyone who wants to do so to comment on things they have discussed – but underline that there is *no obligation* to do so.

Feedback **(3 minutes)**

Outline the topic for the session: the reasons for getting married. The most important reasons are the ones they have themselves, so exploring those comes first.

Why this one?

(15 minutes)

Hand out the first question from Resource sheet 6.

EITHER:

In groups of four **(10 minutes)**

Ask them to spend a couple of minutes each saying why, out of all humanity, they have chosen their partner to marry. What is it about him or her that makes them want to do that? NB: There will be no reporting back, so they only have to say something in front of two other people who are in the same boat.

In the whole group (**5 minutes**)

Did you find the reasons were the same? Similar? Or quite different?

OR:

Ask them to write on a piece of paper (anonymously) three reasons why, out of all humanity, they have chosen their partner. What is it about him or her that makes them want to do that?

Encourage them that light-hearted answers are as good as serious ones.

If they avoid the words 'he' and 'she' it will probably be more fun!

Explain that you will mix up the papers before you read them out!

Individual work (**2 minutes**)

Mix the papers up and get people to read them out, while you put the reasons up on the flip chart or OHP (**5 minutes**)

Note whether the reasons were the same, similar, or quite different.

Ask them whether they recognized their partner's contribution!

General discussion (**8 minutes**)

Introduction to the Preface to the Marriage Service

(5 minutes)

- Explain that the results of the preceding part of the session show why no one can advise anyone else on how to be married. We all have different needs, expectations and fears. Many will have watched *The Good Life*. Tom and Barbara are happily married, and so are Margot and Gerry; but none of them could possibly be married to their 'opposite number' in the other house.
- If they don't know that programme, suggest they think of their favourite soap, and why each of the pairs of partners in those stories is different from all the other pairs. They are already involved in an adventure of getting to know another person better than anyone else in the world – and maybe discovering things about themselves as well.
- But there are probably also some reasons everyone has in common. In the wedding service, there is a section towards the beginning called 'The Preface', which, among other things, sets out three reasons for marriage. In essence, they are 'children, sex and companionship'. How those reasons have been expressed, and the order in which they are listed, has varied through the ages. Read the reasons as they come in *Common Worship*. They are the same in the other orders of service that are still legal, although stated in a different order. The order is not particularly important. As well as being printed here, these reasons can be found on the CD-ROM.

> *The gift of marriage brings husband and wife together*
> *in the delight and tenderness of sexual union*
> *and joyful commitment to the end of their lives.*
> *It is given as the foundation of family life*
> *in which children are [born and] nurtured*
> *and in which each member of the family,*
> *in good times and in bad,*
> *may find strength, companionship and comfort,*
> *and grow to maturity in love.*

- (If time allows, you may like to read also the equivalent parts of the Alternative Preface from *Common Worship* and from *The Book of Common Prayer*; they are also on the CD-ROM.)
- Suggest they think of those three reasons as the legs of a three-legged stool. That is enough to give someone solid support. It may be that sometimes one leg is shorter than the others, but as long as there are three legs, people do not fall down.
- Explain that for the rest of this session they will be exploring those three reasons, and that since *Growing Together* works through topics in alphabetical order, that is how we will discuss them.

Children
(20 minutes)

- Ask them to think back to the 'dream picture' they made in the last session. Did they include children in their dreams (including any either of them may already have), and, in each couple, did each partner include the same number of future children?
- Reflect on the changing shape of marriages:
    - Later age of marriage
    - Smaller numbers of children – because of better contraception
    - More time together as a couple before or after child-rearing, or both!
    - One or both partners may already have children.

Ask them, as a group, to suggest the factors which help people to decide how many children they want and when.

List these factors on a flip chart or OHP and follow up with a general discussion. **(5 minutes)**

Move on to some less happy factors. They have their dream, but might there be a nightmare?

- One couple in six go to the doctor fearing they have a fertility problem (happily, most of these couples do not have a serious problem and find that they can eventually conceive).
- It is useful therefore to face up to how they might feel if that were their situation.
- It is easier to talk about it now, when it isn't a real issue, than when emotions are running high.

Ask them, in their pairs, to talk about how they would feel if they had difficulty conceiving. What would they want to do?

Couples who do not want to have children (or to have any more children) might like instead to talk about what they would do if they found they *had* conceived. Again, underline that this is a private discussion; there will be no reporting back.

Sharing in pairs **(10 minutes)**

Companionship

(20 minutes)

Ask them now to start thinking about companionship, or friendship.

Most couples meet as friends first of all, before they fall in love. For some, that means that friendship gets pushed into second place – being lovers is the task of the moment.

In the end, friendship is the longest lasting of all these three. Being friends is a basic requirement for a good marriage. But what makes a good friend?

Ask them for their thoughts on that.

List elements of friendship on a flip chart or OHP; and general discussion (5 minutes)

Quote the words from Kahlil Gibran's *The Prophet*:

> *And stand together, yet not too near together,*
> *For the pillars of the temple stand apart*
> *And the oak tree and the cypress grow not in each other's shadow.*

How they spend time – together and apart, with friends as well as with each other – is something they all have to negotiate. Sometimes it can be quite surprising to work out just how much time they have together.

Hand out the worksheet in Resource sheet 7.

Explain that on the piece of paper they have they will find four columns, headed 'Alone', 'Apart but with others', 'Together' and 'Together with others', and a week's worth of days. Ask them to think through the last week, since the last session, and tot up roughly how many of their waking hours fell into each of those four categories.

Work in pairs together, in this room.

Work in pairs (5 minutes)

Ask them whether the figures surprise them, and how they feel about them. How do they negotiate the way they spend time together or apart? Is it easy or difficult? How do they keep a balance?

Read to them the story of Bob and Miranda (*Growing Together*, pp. 33–4).

How do they feel about the way that couple handled things? Would it work for them?

General discussion (5 minutes)

Sex

(20 minutes)

The third reason in the Preface is sex.

Cover the following points:

- Sex is God's gift to us and, far from being naughty, it is something holy and wonderful, and to be celebrated. But like any other skill, although it is the most natural thing in the world, it has to be learned; their task as a couple is to be each other's teacher.

- However good their sex education may have been, they need to go on learning from each other, both now and in the future.
- Raise the question of what attitudes to sex couples encountered during their upbringing. For example, did their respective parental homes have the same attitude to sex, and to nudity?
- Reassure them that many couples take time to settle down sexually; that is normal. If problems do persist, however, it is good to seek help earlier rather than later.

Read the stories of Mike and Julie, and Kevin and Mandy (Growing Together, p. 80).

Hand out Resource sheet 8.

This piece of paper has two columns – 'Biggest turn-ons' and 'Biggest turn-offs' – and two sections – 'For me' and 'For you'. Ask everyone to take a couple of minutes now to write what they want to about those (without looking at what their partner is writing!).

Individual work **(3 minutes)**

Sex is intimate and private, so now ask them to go with their own partner again and just compare and share what they have each written. They can then move on to the more general question at the foot of that sheet of paper: 'What does sex add to your whole relationship?' No reporting back!

Sharing in pairs **(12 minutes)**

If timings have gone well, there should be about ten minutes left. If not, you will need to edit or omit all or part of the final section below.

Ending

(10 minutes)

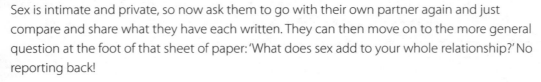

Hand out Resource sheet 4.

Explain that, as last week, they have a piece of paper provided on which they will find two columns, one headed by an exclamation mark, the other by a question mark.

Ask them to jot down *individually*, under the exclamation mark, any new thought (not necessarily a profound one!) that has occurred to them this evening; and under the question mark to put down anything that has raised questions they want to pursue further. Say that there will be an opportunity at the beginning of next week's session, if they want it, to share anything that has come out of this evening, but there will be no pressure to say anything if they prefer not to.

Individual responses (2 minutes)

Ask them to share, with someone *other* than their own partner, any 'exclamation mark' thoughts that have come to them as a result of this evening.

Sharing in pairs (2 minutes)

Then ask them to share with their *real* partner any 'question mark' areas which have come up this evening and which they would like to explore further with each other.

Sharing as couples (2 minutes)

Say that if personal issues have been raised during the session that are causing concern, they should speak to the leader afterwards.

Lastly, ask them to take a minute or two in silence to reflect on all that has been said, both together and privately. Explain that you will then offer all those thoughts to God in a short prayer to close.

Week 3

Communication

Preparation checklist

- A warm room with enough chairs – preferably comfortable ones – for every participant.
- If possible, other spaces to which couples can spread for their private discussions.
- Photocopies of the question in Resource sheet 9. There should be one for each *person*, not one for each couple.
- Photocopies of any worksheets. There should be one for each *person*, not one for each couple.
- Pens
- Paper
- Flip chart or OHP
- CD-player
- Refreshments.

Introduction and non-verbal communication

(10 minutes)

Welcome participants back. Express the hope that, if couples had things they wanted to discuss further with each other, they have found time to do it.

Invite anyone who wants to do so to comment on the things they have discussed, but underline that there is *no obligation* to do so.

Feedback **(3 minutes)**

Outline the topic for this session: communication. Include the following:

- Good communication is a basic skill. Certainly the most common thing people say when they go for marriage counselling is that communications have broken down.
- There are two elements. The first is talking – because if two people do not talk to each other, how can each know what the other one thinks and feels?
- The second skill is listening. If a person is not listening, it will not matter how much someone else says to them; the message will not get through.
- Explain that for the exercises they will do today they will all stay in this room, although they will be working in pairs. Before they do some talking and listening in a moment – and to remind them that words are not the only way to communicate – ask them first to hold their intended's hand, and to take it in turn to express an emotion by the way they hold it. Ask them to close their eyes for this

exercise; otherwise they will also be using facial expressions, which is of course another important way of communicating.

Hand messages (2 minutes)

Next, ask them to see how many emotions they can communicate to each other by means of facial expressions. Ask them to take it in turns, and to check afterwards whether the message has been accurately received.

Facial expressions (2 minutes)

Speaking, hearing and listening

(25 minutes)

Explain that they will do many exercises tonight and that your job will be to keep time for them. So they don't need to worry about keeping an eye on their watches; you will ensure they get messages about when to stop and what to do next.

Ask them first of all find someone other than their partner. Ask them to talk to that person for a minute, non-stop, about what they did yesterday. Both members of each pair are to do this *at the same time* – just talk *at* each other, without attempting to listen to the other one. It's up to them both to keep going.

Simultaneous talk (1 minute)

In the full group, ask: how did that feel? **(2 minutes)**

Now ask everyone to return to work with their own partner. First of all, one person in each couple is to tell a story for two minutes – perhaps about something that happened to them when the other partner wasn't there. The other person is to do their very best to ignore their partner. Suggest they might look the other way; or fiddle with their watch; or whatever they like – but don't pay any attention.

Ignored talk (2 minutes)

Then ask them to reverse roles and do it again.

Ignored talk (2 minutes)

In the full group, ask what that felt like for them.

Now ask for one person in each couple to tell another story, from the distant past – maybe they could talk about their first day at their secondary school, or the day they left school. But it can be a story about anything at all. Again, they have two minutes to tell it. This time, however, the listener should pay full attention, because they will be asked to recall what they have heard.

Careful listening (2 minutes)

Ask for the listener now to recount that story. They have one minute.

Recall (1 minute)

Ask them again to reverse roles, the storyteller becoming the listener. Again they will have two minutes for the story and then a minute for the recounting.

Careful listening (**2 minutes**)

Ask the listener now to recount that story. They have one minute.

Recall (**1 minute**)

Ask participants to share what doing this exercise felt like. You may want to use some of these prompts: Was it easier to be the talker or the listener? What are the things that make listening difficult? What helped you to talk? What did it feel like to hear your story being accurately/ inaccurately retold? Did the things that were missed out matter?

General discussion (**5 minutes**)

Explain that we are now going to take that one stage further. Ask them to recall the two stories they told. Ask them, in pairs, to try to recall not the facts of those stories, but the *emotions* that were being carried by them. What did they think the person talking was *feeling*? They will have just a minute each to try to do that.

Recall of feelings (**2 minutes**)

How easy is it to pick up another person's emotions? How easy do you find it to express them?

General discussion (**3 minutes**)

Other ways of communicating

(15 minutes)

- Remind participants of the ways already discussed in which communication happens. Ask them if they can think of other ways as well.
- Hopefully the group will come up with other things, but if they don't, prompt with things like: body language, clothes, smell (pheromones as well as perfumes – it is something we do naturally), music, lighting, tears, laughter . . .

General discussion (**15 minutes**)

Improving our skills

(30 minutes)

Cover the following points:

- Most people love to be understood and hate it when they are misunderstood.
- We relish having someone's undivided attention, because it affirms that we matter and what we think and say matters. The Children's Society once ran a very perceptive campaign using the slogan 'This child needs a good listening to'. So do we all.

Ask them now to go off in their pairs for half an hour. How they use that time is up to them. Tell them they have 15 minutes each (and you will make a suitable noise to let them all know when it is half-time). What matters here is not *what* they talk about, but *the way* they talk about it.

Suggest each partner picks an issue that concerns them, excites them, puzzles them – *but nothing too major*, because there isn't time to deal with something like that. Talk about it for a while – certainly no more than ten minutes – using all those skills of attentive listening and playing back and reading body language and facial expression, tone of voice, and all the other things that have been mentioned.

Then take a step back, and see how it felt; what helped and what hindered good communication?

Then, when half-time comes, the other partner has the chance to raise *their* issue and deal with it in the same way. Remember, everyone can improve their listening, understanding and talking skills. No one is perfect at it!

Work in pairs **(30 minutes)**

Ending

(10 minutes)

If timings have gone well, there should be about ten minutes left. If not, you will need to edit or omit all or part of this final section.

Hand out Resource sheet 4.

Explain that, as last week, they have a piece of paper provided on which they will find two columns, one headed by an exclamation mark, the other by a question mark.

Ask them to jot down *individually*, under the exclamation mark, any new thought (not necessarily a profound one!) that has occurred to them this evening; and under the question mark to put down anything that has raised questions they want to pursue further. Say that there will be an opportunity at the beginning of next week's session, if they want it, to share anything that has come out of this evening, but there will be no pressure to say anything if they prefer not to.

Individual responses (2 minutes)

Ask them to share with someone *other* than their partner any 'exclamation mark' thoughts which have come to them as a result of this evening.

Sharing in pairs (2 minutes)

Then ask them to share with their *real* partner any 'question mark' areas which have come up this evening and which they would like to explore further with each other.

Sharing as couples (2 minutes)

Say that if any personal issues have been raised during the session which are causing concern, anyone affected should speak to the leader afterwards.

Lastly, ask them to take a minute or two in silence to reflect on all that has been said, together and privately. Explain that you will then offer all those thoughts to God in a short prayer to close.

Conflict

Preparation checklist

- A warm room with enough chairs – preferably comfortable ones – for every participant.
- If possible, other spaces to which couples can spread for their private discussions.
- Photocopies of the questions in Resource sheet 10, cut so each question can be handed out separately. There should be one for each *person*, not one for each couple.
- Photocopies of any worksheets. There should be one for each *person*, not one for each couple.
- Pens
- Paper
- Flip chart or OHP
- CD-player
- Refreshments.

Introduction

(5 minutes)

Welcome them back. Express the hope that, if couples had things they wanted to discuss further with each other, they have found time to do it.

Invite anyone who wants to to so to comment on things they have discussed, but underline that there is *no obligation* to do so.

Feedback **(3 minutes)**

Outline the topic for the session: conflict.

Underline that this is not being negative; it is facing up to the fact that being married is not always easy. That does not reflect on the reality of their love – it reflects the fact that a marriage is two individuals trying to work as a team.

Being realistic

(20 minutes)

Hand out Resource sheet 11.

This worksheet has two columns, with lots of blank lines for them to fill in.

Ask the participants, as couples, to fill in as many lines as they can as quickly as they can. Each partner has a column, so they should put their name at the top of it. Ask them to think of as many ways as they can in which they are different from each other. The paper gives a start with the most obvious: one is male, the other female.

Include the following points:

- People sometimes say 'We have our differences', meaning that they disagree.
- But differences are not necessarily a problem – in fact they can be very positive. If one of you was not male and the other female, you wouldn't be here tonight!

Ask them, when they have filled in as many differences as they want, then to circle the ones which are a plus factor for them – differences that are a good thing – and to put a square round the ones which are a problem, or a potential problem for them – differences that are a bad thing. Point out that there will probably be several differences that are neither one thing nor the other – or maybe both!

Work in pairs **(7 minutes)**

Hand out Resource sheet 3.

Explain they now have another piece of paper with four rough graphs on it. Cover the following points:

- The first three graphs are unrealistic maps of how a marriage will be. The first represents ever-increasing bliss; the second represents ever-increasing misery. The third represents no change at all – everything just as it is for ever.
- Explain that if any of those is how their relationships are, then they have a problem.
- The last one is the reality.
- There will be ups and downs in everyone's relationships; the vital thing is how they are handled.
- Ask them to have a go at plotting, individually, on the back of that sheet a graph of how they as individuals see their relationship so far. Hopefully there haven't been any major downs, but there will almost certainly have been little blips – maybe stresses caused from outside when a house purchase fell through, or when there was a bereavement.

Individual graph plotting **(3 minutes)**

Ask them then to go with their partner and compare notes and talk about what they have drawn, and whether they see the ups and down in the same way. **(7 minutes)**

Recognizing our skills

(10 minutes)

Refer to the chapter 'Conflict' in *Growing Together*, which uses the analogy of a first-aid box. Having one in the house is very sensible – but it is important to know where it is and what is in it. Then, when a crisis comes and you have cut your finger, you know where you can get help. The vast majority of the conflicts we have in relationships are going to be solved by our relationship's first-aid box – that collection of bits and pieces we have acquired that we know can help.

Ask them to share some of the kinds of things that might be in it. What are the everyday ways in which people can get over glitches in their relationships? What helps them to make up and move on?

List a few possibilities on a flip chart or OHP.

Underline that those are a few things in general. What will be more important will be the things *they* have in their personal first-aid box.

Ask them to work in couples to make their own personal list of the things that help them get through bad moments. If they are willing to share some of them when everyone comes together again, that would be useful.

Hand out the first question from Resource sheet 10.

Work in pairs (**5 minutes**)

Sharing ideas (adding to the list on a flip chart/OHP) (**3 minutes**)

Outside help

(10 minutes)

If first aid doesn't work, we usually seek outside help from the doctor. In relationship terms, the first line of help may be family or friends.

   Ask them to list the pluses and minuses of using family and friends if there is a problem.

List these on a flip chart or OHP. (**5 minutes**)

If they don't mention it themselves, include the fact that some families and friends will not be helpful. It may be the nature of the problem, or the nature of the family. They reasonably may not want to worry their families with their problems.

   If a medical problem really *is* a crisis, then people forget the first-aid box and the GP and go off to the nearest A&E department.

   Ask them to list what the equivalent places might be for a crisis in a relationship.

List on flip chart or OHP, prompting if necessary: clergy, counsellor, financial adviser, doctor, etc. (**5 minutes**)

Facing difficult facts

(10 minutes)

Cover the following points:

- Marriages can be dangerous things.
- Statistics show that one in every three women will suffer domestic violence at some point in her life.
- The average victim does not go to the police until there have been 33 occasions of violence.

- One in every seven men will suffer domestic violence, and men are also much less likely to report such happenings.
- Once violence has happened – or nearly happened – it changes the way people think of each other. The Bible talks about perfect love casting out fear, but unfortunately the reverse is also true – fear can cast out love, and violence breeds fear.

Ask them, in pairs, to talk about these statistics, and what they make them feel. It is all about anger; so ask them, when they have talked about the issue in general, then also to talk about how each of them handles anger: something that we all have, and that may be justified. But although anger can be justifiable, violence never can.

Hand out the second question from Resource sheet 10.

Work in pairs (**10 minutes**)

What would you do?

(25 minutes)

Hand out Resource sheet 12.

Explain that they have been given four situations. They won't have time to look at all of them in this session, but there is always the chance to look at the others at home. The questions are the same for each situation:

1 What is the obvious problem?
2 Are there other problems that might lie behind this one?
3 Do you think the couple should be able to solve it for themselves?
- If so, what can *each* of them do to contribute to the solution?
- If not, what sort of outside help might they look for?

Ask them to work in pairs on one or more of the situations for 20 minutes.

Ending

(10 minutes)

If timings have gone well, there should be about ten minutes left. If not, you will need to edit or omit all or part of this final section.

Hand out Resource sheet 4.

Explain that, as last week, they have a piece of paper provided on which they will find two columns, one headed by an exclamation mark, the other by a question mark.

Ask them to jot down *individually*, under the exclamation mark, any new thought (not necessarily a profound one!) that has occurred to them this evening; and under the question mark to put down anything that has raised questions they want to pursue further. Say that there will be an opportunity at the beginning of next week's session, if they want it, to share anything that has come out of this evening, but there will be no pressure to say anything if they prefer not to.

Individual responses (2 minutes)

Ask them to share with someone *other* than their partner any 'exclamation mark' thoughts that have come to them as a result of this evening.

Sharing in pairs (2 minutes)

And then ask them to share with their *real* partner any 'question mark' areas which have come up this evening and which they would like to explore further with each other.

Sharing as couples (2 minutes)

Say that if personal issues have been raised during the session, which are causing concern, anyone affected should speak to the leader afterwards.

Lastly, ask them to take a minute or two in silence to reflect on all that has been said, together and privately. Explain that you will then offer all those thoughts to God in a short prayer to close.

Week 5
Spiritual issues

Preparation checklist

- A warm room with enough chairs – preferably comfortable ones – for every participant.
- If possible, other spaces to which couples can spread for their private discussions.
- Photocopies of the questions in Resource sheet 13, cut so that each question can be handed out separately. There should be one for each *person*, not one for each couple.
- Photocopies of any worksheets. There should be one for each *person*, not one for each couple.
- Pens
- Paper
- Flip chart or OHP
- CD-player
- Refreshments.

Introduction

(3 minutes)

Welcome them back. Express the hope that, if they had things they wanted to discuss further with each other, they have found time to do it.

Invite anyone who wants to do so to comment on things they have discussed, but underline that there is *no obligation* to do so.

Feedback (**3 minutes**)

Outline the topic for the session: spiritual issues.

Beliefs

(10 minutes)

Christians say we are one unit, made up of body, mind and soul. All those parts need to be married.

Couples vary a lot in how much they know about their partner's beliefs.

Ask the participants to imagine a line running diagonally from one corner of the room to the other. Explain that if they are totally confident that they know their partner's beliefs, they need to be right in whichever corner you define for that view. If they are totally confident that they have not the faintest idea what their partner's beliefs are, they need to be right in the opposite corner. Most of them will want to place themselves somewhere along the imaginary line between the two. Ask them to go to the appropriate position now.

Place themselves on imaginary line.

As they stand in those places, ask them to think for a moment *why* they are where they are. What are the things that make them confident or otherwise? If they are in the middle, *why* are they not very sure?

Ask them to return to their seats to share their thoughts.

General discussion

If the participants do not mention these points, suggest that sometimes people find it difficult to put beliefs into words, or are afraid of being laughed at or having their beliefs challenged.

Suggest also that part of the 'intimacy' of marriage is not having 'no go' areas.

Faith matters

(15 minutes)

- The fact that they decided to get married in church was bound to open up questions of faith. Point out that among the present group there are probably both people who are regular worshippers and people who have never have set foot in the church. Somehow or other, they have all come to the decision that a church wedding is what they want.

- Ask them each to write on a piece of paper *their own* reason for getting married in church: not their reason as a couple; not their partner's reason; but *their own*. Ask them to be ruthlessly honest – if the reason is to keep their parents quiet, or whatever, then they should say so! Assure them that you will mix up all the pieces of paper before reading them out.

Individual work **(2 minutes)**

Sharing (on a flip chart or OHP if desired) **(3 minutes)**

Sometimes people think it is strange that people who don't usually go to church want to have their wedding there. Ask them to imagine they are being interviewed for a TV programme by someone who thinks like that. What are the things they would want to say in reply?

Ask them to go in their pairs to do two things. First of all prepare their 'interview'. They might like to jot down some bullet points they would want to include in their replies – but assure them it is a private document and they won't have to share it.

The second task is to write a prayer that will be true to where they stand in matters of faith. There is a famous prayer that went: 'O God, if there is a God, help me to save my soul, if I have a soul.' Again, this prayer is private and not for publication. Point out to them, however, that *Common Worship* does give couples permission to write their own prayers for the service, if they wish.

Hand out the first question from Resource sheet 13.

Work in pairs **(15 minutes)**

Cover the following points:

- Everyone is on a faith journey of some kind.
- We are all believers or non-believers; we all have a religious 'position' now.
- Those positions may change during the time they are married, and any change will affect both of them.
- There will be other faith decisions to make: for example, whether any children will be baptized.

Priorities and money

(25 minutes)

- Ask the participants to think about what are the most important things in life to them. Explain they are going to do an exercise that will show up what is true for them.
- In order to be clear what their task is, suggest having a practice run together on the OHP or flip chart. You will need to have prepared a grid like the one on Resource sheet 14. The easiest way to demonstrate its use is to answer it for yourself, if you are willing! First of all, compare row 1 with row 2. Put a mark in the first thin column against the one that is the more important. Now compare row 1 with row 3, and put a mark in that same column to show which is more important out of those two items. Do that all the way down, comparing row 1 with each of the other rows. Now take row 2 (forget the row above) and do the same, comparing it with rows 3, 4 and so on, and mark those results in the second thin column. Then take row 3 and compare it with all the rows below, in the third column. Do that all the way through. Then add up the number of marks in each row. The one with the highest number of marks against it is the first priority.
- Ask if everyone is clear what they have to do. There are seven items listed. They might want to add one or two more for themselves.

Ask them to do the exercise individually first of all, and then to compare notes to see whether their priorities are the same. If they add their results for each row together, they will then get their joint order of priorities. Is this the same as their individual ones, or different? Explain they have ten minutes to do that and talk about it.

Work in pairs (**10 minutes**)

Cover the following points:

- Money is another way of working out what our deepest priorities are.
- How we spend our money – or at least the part of it left when the mortgage/rent/council tax/utility bills have been paid – reveals the things that are most important to us.
- Attitudes to money can often be rooted in childhood.
- Read the story of Michael and Judith (*Growing Together*, pp. 66–7).

- Suggest that at home they look at their priority list and see how it compares with how they spend their money. Point out that the two will not match, because something that is a high priority might demand little cash, and something much lower down the list might be quite expensive.

Hand out the second question from Resource sheet 13. These are spiritual issues as well as practical ones, because they are about our deepest values. Suggest that if they don't manage to answer all the questions in the time available, they do so at home later.

Work in pairs (**10 minutes**)

Questions of life and death

(25 minutes)

Death is a subject most people run away from. (You will find one or two light-hearted stories in the 'script' in Resource sheet 22 that may be useful in broaching this subject.)
  Ask them to decide what words they would like on their tombstone.

Individual work and then shared in pairs (**3 minutes**)

- Ask them to think about the implications of 'till death do us part'.
- Have they made a will, or are they going to do so?
- Do they want to be buried or cremated?
- What are their feelings about organ donation?

Explain they will now have 15 minutes to talk through how they both feel about these issues and to share their experiences of bereavement, from the death of childhood pets onwards. How do they cope with these eternal questions of life and death?

Hand out question 3 from Resource sheet 13.

Work in pairs (**15 minutes**)

Ending

(10 minutes)

If timings have gone well, there should be about ten minutes left. If not, you will need to edit or omit all or part of this final section.

Hand out Resource sheet 4.

Explain that, as last week, they have a piece of paper provided on which they will find two columns, one headed by an exclamation mark, the other by a question mark.
  Ask them to jot down *individually*, under the exclamation mark, any new thought (not necessarily a profound one!) that has occurred to them this evening; and under the question mark to put down anything that has raised questions they want to pursue further. Say that there will be an opportunity at the beginning of next week's session, if they want it, to share anything that has come out of this evening, but there will be no pressure to say anything if they prefer not to.

Individual responses (2 minutes)

Ask them to share with someone *other* than their partner any 'exclamation mark' thoughts that have come to them as a result of this evening.

Sharing in pairs (2 minutes)

Then ask them to share with their *real* partner any 'question mark' areas that have come up this evening and which they would like to explore further with each other.

Sharing as couples (2 minutes)

Say that if personal issues that are causing concern have been raised during the session, anyone affected should speak to the leader afterwards.

Lastly, ask them to take a minute or two in silence to reflect on all that has been said, together and privately. Explain that you will then offer all those thoughts to God in a short prayer to close.

Week 6
Us and them

Preparation checklist

- A warm room with enough chairs – preferably comfortable ones – for every participant
- If possible, other spaces to which couples can spread for their private discussions
- Photocopies of any worksheets. There should be one for each *person*, not one for each couple.
- Pens
- Paper
- Flip chart or OHP
- CD-player
- Refreshments.

Introduction

(5 minutes)

Welcome them back. Express the hope that, if they had things they wanted to discuss further with each other, they have found time to do it.

Invite anyone who wants to to comment on things they have discussed – but underline that there is *no obligation* to do so.

Feedback **(3 minutes)**

Outline the topic for the session: us and them.

Who does what?

(20 minutes)

Read the story of Colin and Bernice (*Growing Together*, pp. 74–5).

Hand out Resource sheet 15. This sheet lists a number of household tasks and has some blank spaces as well. Ask the participants to brainstorm some other things that *someone* has to do in every home; everyone can then fill these additions in on their worksheets.

Brainstorm ideas.

Ask the participants now to stay together in the main meeting-room, but to work as couples. Ask them each to fill in on their sheet who *used* to do each task in their home when they were children. Next, ask them to put down who does them in their current home – or who they will expect to do it, if they are not yet living together. They should then compare notes and talk about whether the work is divided up in a way that they both feel comfortable with.

Explain that in the feedback session afterwards we shall simply list the things that caused the most arguments!

Work in pairs (**5 minutes**)

Reporting back (**5 minutes**)

Those have been practical things. But there will be other ways in which they divide labour. One partner may be a saver and the other a spender. Or one may be a good decision maker, while the other finds it hard to come to any conclusion.

Ask them to take ten minutes exploring the other ways in which they share their strengths and weaknesses. Say that this time there will be no reporting back.

Work in pairs (**10 minutes**)

The wider family

(20 minutes)

Getting married joins together two families, as well as two individuals. But every family is different, and affects how that happens.

Tell the stories of Greg and Jo, and of Kevin and Maggie (*Growing Together*, pp. 58–9).

Ask the participants to draw a family map (flip chart paper would be useful for this). It doesn't matter how they draw it, as long as both members of each couple understand what it means.

Hand out the Family Map example sheet (*Resource sheet 16*) and a blank sheet of paper.

Show them how the example sheet is just using some of the conventional symbols to guide them. They might want to place people nearer to them or further away from them according to how much they see them; or to put brackets round people if they are not in touch with them at all.

Ask that when they have drawn their map, with however many people they want to include, they have a look at it and see what similarities and differences there are between their two families of origin. Do those similarities and differences affect the way they each think about the wider family?

Work in pairs (**15 minutes**)

The place we live in

(20 minutes)

The *Common Worship* Marriage Service talks about the effects of marriage being wider even than individual families: 'It enriches society and strengthens community.'

Ask the participants to share ideas about how they think that can happen.

Brainstorm (**10 minutes**)

(If they are not mentioned by others, add ideas about how happy homes make for happier places of work, better health, more energy to give to others, capacity to care for others, etc. It is even true that some of the current need to build more houses is partly because of the numbers of people living alone through the failure of relationships. That affects the environment for everyone.)

Last of all, ask them, in pairs, to share together what very specific things they think they can give to their community life at the moment. The amount of time and energy people have will change as work and family demands change, so it is very much a question of what is possible *now*. Does either of them do anything to help community life, through voluntary groups, etc? Is that something one or both of them might consider? It is part of their marriage, whether or not they are both involved – if one of them goes to do something, the other must be happy to let them go!

Work in pairs (**10 minutes**)

Ending

(**25 minutes**)

Hand out *two* copies of Resource sheet 4 for each group member.

Explain that, as last week, they have a piece of paper provided on which they will find two columns, one headed by an exclamation mark, the other by a question mark.

Ask them to jot down *individually*, under the exclamation mark, any new thought (not necessarily a profound one!) that has occurred to them this evening; and under the question mark to put down anything that has raised questions they want to pursue further.

Individual responses (**2 minutes**)

Ask them this week to share *both* lists with their *real* partner.

Sharing as couples (**3 minutes**)

Explain that, because the next session will be very different, when we will be looking at the wedding day itself and the choices and decisions they have to make about it, this is really the last chance they have for any general questions or comments they want to make about the last six sessions. Ask them, as couples, to jot down together the 'question mark' and 'exclamation mark' points that have come out of *the course as a whole*.

Work in pairs (**5 minutes**)

Offer the opportunity to share any of the things that they have put on that last sheet.

General discussion (**15 minutes**)

Say that if any personal issues have been raised during the session and are causing concern, anyone affected should speak to the leader afterwards.

Lastly, ask them to take a minute or two in silence to reflect on all that has been said, together and privately. Explain that you will then offer all those thoughts to God in a short prayer to close.

Week 7

The wedding day

How this session is organized, and the timings, will depend on your local situation. You may want it to be in church, so that the organist can play and the flower arrangers can show where flowers can be placed, and so on. The bullet lists provide you with an aide-memoire of the areas that need to be considered. Some of them may be irrelevant in your situation – but there may be others you will need to add.

The timings for this session will depend on the other people you involve in it. It could be covered in the hour suggested, but it is likely there will be many questions, so it is probably better to aim for a 90-minute session, as in the previous weeks, or to end with some refreshments to round things off.

Resource sheet 17 is a worksheet that can be used as it is or adapted to suit local usage.

Making decisions about the wedding

(50 minutes)

This is a couple's own day – and the choices are theirs. So they should personalize as much as they can. They may also want to involve other people in what happens. They do need, however, to check with the vicar everything they would like to do.

Order of service

Strictly speaking, there are three orders of service that are legal: the 1662 Book of Common Prayer, the 1928 Prayer Book (Series 1) and *Common Worship* (2000). In practice *Common Worship* probably has everything they might want, including a form of wedding with Holy Communion, which is an option any couples who are regular communicants might want to consider. It doesn't necessarily add a lot of time to the service.

Choreography

Explain that couples need to decide . . .

- Who walks in with whom
- When (and where) people should stand or sit
- On 'giving away' or alternatives
- Where the registers are signed
- Etc.

Hymns

Explain that . . .

- There is space in the service for four, but they do not have to have that many.
- The most important thing is that people know the hymns chosen. It's embarrassing for everyone if the vicar has to sing a solo!
- Some fit in one place better than another – so, for example, a hymn about vows goes well at the point when they are about to make theirs; or a hymn which is a prayer just before the prayers. It is also generally best to go out on the most joyous note.
- It's also important for them to check that the tune the organist has in mind is also the tune they are expecting. Some popular hymns, such as 'Love divine' or 'At the name of Jesus', have more than one well-known tune.
- Copyright issues need to be checked.
- It's a good idea to start thinking now! People often pick up ideas when they go to church on Sundays, or to other people's weddings.
- Not all churches have organists who can play anything that is put in front of them. Discussion with the clergy is important, in case there are any local restrictions to bear in mind.

Readings

- Who? This is a good opportunity to involve other people, but do stress the need for readers to practise, particularly if there are tricky names in the readings chosen. (Balaam, for example.)
- What? At least one of the readings must be from the Bible. There are 26 suggestions in *Common Worship* (but they can choose others if they wish).
- Take care to read all the suggested Bible readings, and then cut them down to a short list. Why do these particular readings speak to them?
- Share with the group one or two of the less well-known readings: for example, the one from the Song of Solomon (sometimes called 'the Song of Songs'). Explain it is a really quite erotic poem, which talks about God's love in terms of human passion. The reading doesn't include the parts about the beloved's breasts being like twin fawns, or clusters of grapes, or the man's legs being like alabaster columns set upon bases of gold. This is the bit that it does use: they need to think of a woman hiding behind the lattice window of a Middle Eastern house, with the lover whispering through the window. (Incidentally, it does say in another place that he has arrived there bounding like a young gazelle across the desert!) This is how it goes . . .
- Read the Song of Solomon passage (the text is on Resource sheet 19 and also on the CD-ROM).
- The second is from the Apocrypha – the books from Old Testament times that were left out of some versions of the Bible. This one is from the book of Tobit.
- Read the Tobit passage (the text is on Resource sheet 19 and also on the CD-ROM).
- Explain that the context of that one is rather fun. The couple are praying before

their first night together. But Sarah has been previously given in marriage to seven other men. Unfortunately, before the marriage was consummated, they were all killed by a demon called Asmodeus. Now, people were as sceptical about the reality of demons then as they are today, and they quite reasonably said it was Sarah who had killed off the men. Tobias is very smitten with Sarah, but he has a meeting with the Archangel Raphael, and after another curious incident when a huge fish tries to swallow Tobias's foot when he washes it in the Tigris, he is told by the angel to catch the fish and eat the flesh, but to keep the gall, heart and liver, because they are useful in dealing with demons. So, come his first night with Sarah, when they are obviously both on edge that he might be Victim Number Eight, he takes the precaution of burning these bits of old fish guts as a way of dealing with Asmodeus – which works. Apparently it smells so bad he takes off to Upper Egypt, where Raphael deals with him once and for all.

- Make sure the reader has the right translation – and knows which one will be on the lectern at the service.
- Non-biblical readings are very personal and entirely optional. The most important thing is that what is chosen means something to the couple. All of these need to be OK'd with the vicar. Some brave brides and grooms have written something themselves.

Prayers

- Yet again, a time when couples can make the service very much their own.
- One set of prayers is printed in the main text, but there are many others in *Common Worship: Pastoral Services*. The Marriage Service does not reprint all the alternatives. The idea generally is that they choose one of the longer ones (with the 'response' style) or one from each of the sections of short ones.
- Prayers from elsewhere can also be used.
- Or couples can write their own.

Music

- Music sets the tone and is an important part of the service. There are three basic places to have it:
  - Entry
  - Registers – probably 5–7 minutes' worth
  - Exit
- Organ music is normal – but do make sure that the pieces chosen will suit both the building and the organ. People are sometimes led astray by listening to discs. It is also important to check that the organist can play the pieces chosen!
- Recordings may be possible if a system to play them is available.
- Is live music from friends or family an option?

Oddments

- Banns
- Fees
- Confetti
- Photos and/or videos
- Other practical issues

Ending

(10 minutes)

- Thank them for coming
- Invite final questions
- Give out books
- Use the prayer below to end.

> *There are so many choices:*
> *venues and menus,*
> *dresses and tresses,*
> *shades and bridesmaids,*
> *cars and guitars,*
> *houses and blouses,*
> *speeches and preachers;*
> *It is so easy to over-spend, to lose all sense of proportion.*
> *Help us to plan not only for the day, but for the rest of our life.*
> *Help us to choose the best things:*
> *faith*
> *hope*
> *love.*

(Andrew Body, from *Pocket Prayers for Marriage*)

There is an audio file on the CD-ROM of Andrew reading a concluding prayer, which you may wish to use at the end of this session.

How have we grown?
A reunion course

A scripted version, for those who prefer it, can be found at Resource sheet 23 and on the CD-ROM.

Although this has been set out as one 90-minute session, it could easily be expanded if required. If it is run at a weekend, it could be combined with a lunch.

Outline

- Introduction (**10–15 minutes**)
- Things move on (**25 minutes**)
- How are the reasons for marriage developing? (**30 minutes**)
- Current dreams (**10 minutes**)
- Saying 'Thank you' (**10 minutes**)

Introduction

(**10–15 minutes**)

Each couple should be asked in advance to bring with them a picture or an object that reminds them of their wedding or honeymoon.

Most of them have been married between nine months and a year now. Ask everyone to re-introduce themselves, by giving:

- Name
- When they were married
- A comment on the photo or object they have brought.

Things move on

(**25 minutes**)

Ask them to share two of the most important things that have happened to them during the time they have been married.

Group discussion (**10 minutes**)

- Explain that those are things that have happened *to* them. The next task is to have some time in private to identify three things for each of them. These are private discussions – no reporting back.
- Hand out the first three questions from Resource sheet 20.

- Something that has been a surprise – why was that?
- Something that has been better than expected – why was that?
- Something that has been a disappointment – why was that?

Work in pairs (**15 minutes**)

How are the reasons for marriage developing?

(**30 minutes**)

The wedding service identified three reasons for getting married: companionship and friendship; sex; and children.

Ask them as couples to take stock of how those three things have changed and developed. How are things different between them from before they were married? Why have they changed? Are those changes all good? If not, what can they do about it?

They have half an hour, so divide the time between those three things as you choose.

Hand out the final question from Resource sheet 20.

Work in pairs (**30 minutes**)

Current dreams

(**10 minutes**)

Alexander Solzhenitsyn said that marriage was like riding a bicycle – you have to keep moving forward, or you wobble and fall off. So we need to go on having dreams and making them come true if we can.

Ask them what are their dreams for the next year? Are there any ways in which the group could go on supporting each other? Would they like to meet again?

Group discussion (**10 minutes**)

Saying 'Thank you'

(**10 minutes**)

Use a simple form of the service of Thanksgiving for Marriage in *Common Worship Pastoral Services*. It can be found at Resource sheet 18 and on the CD-ROM.

RESOURCE SHEET  **1**

Questions for the one-day course

- What are the good and bad things that come from your experience in the past? What are the things about the marriages you have been part of as children that you would want to be the same in your own marriage? What are the things you would want to be different? You may also like to consider whether your ideas about those things are the same as your partner's, or different from theirs.

- Do you expect getting married to make a difference to you, or not? If so, what difference will it make? If not, why not? This is not an easy thing to tease out. If you say 'No', then you may want to explain why you *do* want to get married. If you say 'Yes', then what does that say about the development of your relationship, and how it might move on?

- What does sex add to your whole relationship?

- How you would feel if you had difficulty conceiving – and what would you want to do? If you are a couple who do not want to have children (or to have any more children), you may like instead to talk about what you would do if you found you *had* conceived.

- Compare notes and talk about what you have drawn on your 'graph', and whether you see the ups and down the same way.

- Then think about the skills you have that help you cope with the less good moments, the irritations and crossed wires that happen. How do you get through those – how do you make up? What are the 'first-aid things' that help bandage your relationship when it gets a bruise?

- Imagine you are being interviewed on TV about why you want to get married in church. What would you say?

RESOURCE SHEET ②

'Us in 10 years' time'

The shape of ups and downs

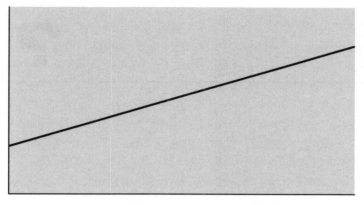

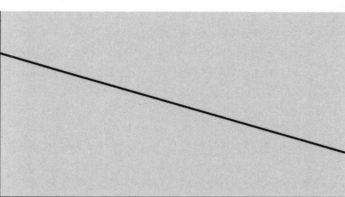

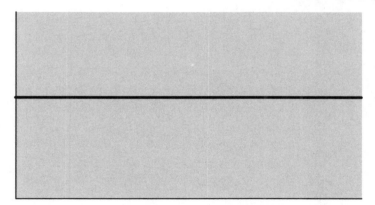

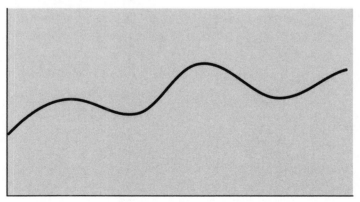

Weekly response sheet

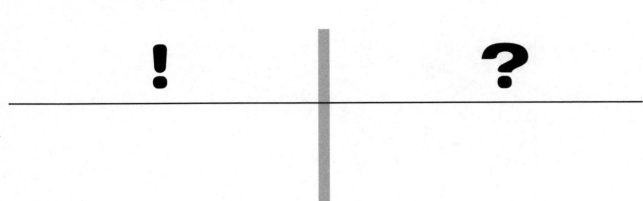

Questions for Week 1 of the seven-week course

- What are the good and bad things that come from your experience in the past? What are the things about the marriages you have been part of as children which you would want to be the same in your marriage, and what are the things you would want to be different? You may like to consider whether your ideas about those things are the same as your partner's, or different from theirs.

- How do your 'Us in 10 years' time' pictures compare? Are your dreams the same? How does that make you feel?

- Do you expect getting married to make a difference to you, or not? If so, what difference will it make? If not, why not? This is not an easy thing to tease out. If you say 'No', then you may want to explain why you *do* want to get married. If you say 'Yes', then what does that say about the development of your relationship, and how it might move on?

Questions for Week 2 of the seven-week course

EITHER:

- Why, out of all humanity, have you chosen this one to marry? What is it about him or her that makes you want to do that? See how much you can embarrass each other!

OR:

- Write on a piece of paper, anonymously, three reasons why, out of all humanity, you have chosen this one to marry. What is it about him or her that makes you want to do that?

- How you would feel if you had difficulty conceiving – and what would you want to do? If you are a couple who do not want to have children (or to have any more children), you may like instead to talk about what you would do if you found you *had* conceived.

RESOURCE SHEET  **7**

Together and apart

	Alone		*Apart but with others*		*Together*		*Together but with others*
Sunday							
Monday							
Tuesday							
Wednesday							
Thursday							
Friday							
Saturday							

Turn-ons and turn-offs

	Biggest turn-ons	Biggest turn-offs
For me:		
For you:		

What does sex add to your whole relationship?

Question for Week 3 of the seven-week course

■ Pick an issue that concerns you, excites you, puzzles you – but *nothing too major*, because there isn't time to deal with something like that. Talk about it for a while – certainly no more than ten minutes – using all those skills of attentive listening and playing back and reading body language and facial expression, tone of voice, and all the other things we have mentioned. Then take a step back and see how it felt: what helped, and what hindered good communication. Then, when half-time comes, your partner has the chance to raise *their* issue, and you deal with it in the same way.

Questions for Week 4 of the seven-week course

■ Think about the skills you have that help you cope with the less good moments, the irritations and crossed wires that happen. How do you get through those? How do you make up? What are the 'first-aid things' that help bandage your relationship when it gets a bruise?

■ Talk about the statistics about domestic violence, and how they make you feel. It is all about anger; so when you have talked about the issue in general, please talk about how each of you handles anger.

Differences

NAME: _____   **NAME:** _____

	Male	**Female**
1	_____	_____
2	_____	_____
3	_____	_____
4	_____	_____
5	_____	_____
6	_____	_____
7	_____	_____
8	_____	_____
9	_____	_____
10	_____	_____
11	_____	_____

Four situations

1   What is the obvious problem?
2   Are there other problems that might lie behind it?
3   Do you think this couple should be able to solve the situation for themselves?
   ■   If so, what can each of them do to contribute to the solution?
   ■   If not, what sort of outside help might they look for?

John and Joanna

They have been married for six months. Joanna comes from a home that was always neat and tidy, where everything happened like clockwork. John's family is at best 'chaotic' – always in a mess, and nothing organized.

They each behave in the same way as the homes they come from. Joanna is frustrated by John's messiness, and he is frustrated by her wanting things to be 'just so'.

Jim and Sally

Jim and Sally live at quite a distance from both sets of parents. Jim's working day is usually 7.30 a.m. to 7.00 p.m. Sally used to work close to their home, and was there to get an evening meal ready.

Now, they have a baby, and Sally feels lonely. She rings her mother to moan, but her mother is too far away to be of practical help. When Jim comes home he is often greeted with tears; so he makes excuses to stay in town with his friends from work.

Tom and Lucy

Tom and Lucy have been married for some months, but have lived together for several years. At a party, an attractive man flirts with Lucy; she enjoys the attention he is giving her and spends most of the evening with him. Tom is aware of what is happening.

When they get home, Lucy is full of fun and wants to make love. Tom is quiet, pushes her away and curls up on the edge of the bed. Lucy complains that he is no fun these days.

Kevin and Helen

Kevin and Helen have been married for three years. He comes from a large family and is looking forward to having children of his own. Helen is hoping for a promotion at work and doesn't think this is a good time to start a family. Kevin says she is turning into a career woman and will never want to have children.

RESOURCE SHEET 13

Questions for Week 5 of the seven-week course

■ Imagine you are being interviewed on TV about why you want to be married in church. What would you say?

Then write a really honest prayer to use in the service.

■ How do you make financial decisions and how do you handle your money? Do you have a joint account, two separate accounts, three accounts, or keep your money under the bed? How do you budget? In particular, do you budget to give money away? Are there things you both care about enough to put into your regular budget?

■ Have you made wills, or are you going to do so? Do you want to be buried or cremated? What are your experiences of bereavement, from the death of childhood pets onwards? How do you cope with these eternal questions of life and death?

RESOURCE SHEET (14)

Priorities

Prioritizing by rank

Features to be prioritized are listed in the left hand column (one per row with spaces to add your own). Compare row 1 with row 2. Put a mark against whichever is more important using the first narrow column (A). Compare row 1 with row 3 and mark, row 1 with row 4, etc. to bottom of list. Then compare row 2 against each subsequent row (use second narrow column for results). Continue stepping through each row until each item has been compared against those below. Add up the number of marks for each row. The row with the most marks has the highest priority. If several people do the exercise their results can be added up to get a group ranking.

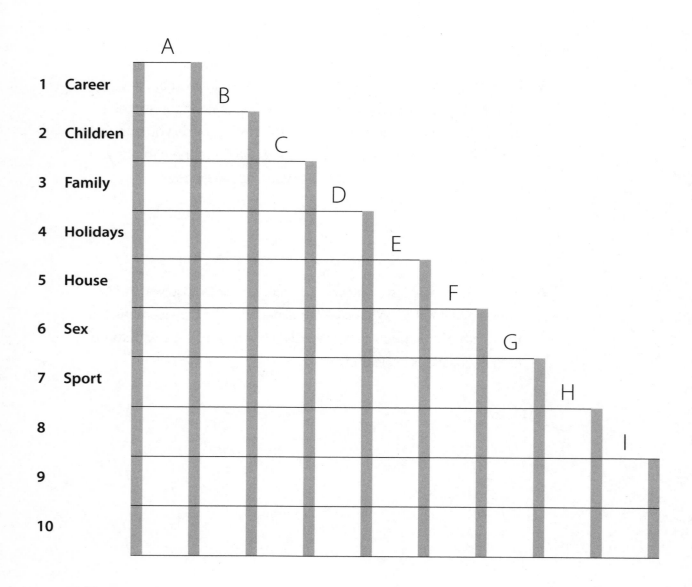

Household tasks

Task	Childhood home	Our home
Shopping		
Cooking		
Putting out rubbish		
Hoovering		
Cleaning the loo		
Washing up		
Laundry		
Ironing		
Paying bills		
Deciding on holidays		
Writing Christmas cards		
Cleaning the car		
Gardening		
Going to parents' evenings		
Disciplining the children		
?		
?		
?		

Family map

Simon has one brother (unmarried), one sister (married with children).

His parents are divorced.

Sally is an only child and her mother is dead.

Her father now lives with someone else, but is not married.

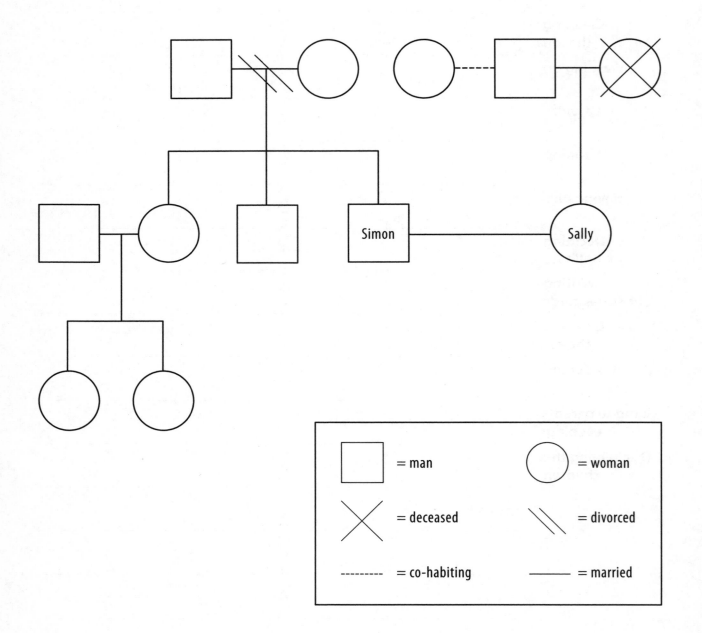

☐	= man		◯	= woman
✕	= deceased		⫽	= divorced
---------	= co-habiting		————	= married

The wedding service

(Page references are to the *Common Worship* Marriage Service booklet.)

Music before the service

Do you want to choose the music played *before* the service begins, or to leave the choice to the organist?

We leave it to the organist
We would like:

Are there any special announcements you would like made before the service?

Please announce:

The Entrance

Are you walking in as a couple, or is the bride coming in alone, supported by her father, mother, or someone else?

We will walk in together
The bride will enter with:

What music will you use at this point?

Music at the entrance:

The Welcome

All the words on page 2 will be used, unless you specify otherwise.

We will use all the words on page 2:
Yes/No

What hymn will you sing at this point? (Please see the note at the back of this leaflet about choosing hymns.)

Hymn

The Preface

The Preface on page 3 will normally be used, unless you ask for the one on page 15.

We want the Preface on page 3 / page 15

What names do you want to be called in the Preface? You may prefer your 'usual' name rather than the formal one, e.g. Chris and Jo rather than Christopher and Joanna.

Please use

and

The Declarations

Do you want to use the declarations on page 4, or the *Book of Common Prayer* text, which reads:

We want to use page 4 / BCP text

> *N, wilt thou have this woman to thy wedded wife, to live together according to God's law in the holy estate of matrimony? Wilt thou love her, comfort her, honour and keep her, in sickness and in health; and, forsaking all other, keep thee only unto her, so long as ye both shall live? (etc.)*

Do you want to use just your first name or your Christian names in full at this point?

Please use

and

Who is going to make the first declaration?

Bride / Groom

The Readings

There must be at least one reading from the Bible (see pages 16–28 for suggestions). But you can choose another biblical reading apart from those suggestions, if you wish.

Our readings will be
i)

read by:

ii)

read by:

If you want an additional reading from other sources (e.g. a poem), that is open for discussion. You will find some popular ideas in the *Additional Readings* booklet.

We would also like

read by:

What hymn will you sing at this point?

Hymn

The Marriage

The traditional 'giving away' ceremony happens at this point, if you wish. As an alternative, you can use the declarations by the families on page 39, para. 6.

We would like to use
    the giving away
    the declaration
    neither

The Vows

There are alternatives to the page 6 vows on pages 29–30. Form 1 on page 29 includes the word 'obey'. Form 2 is the form of vows from the 'old service' and can include 'obey' if you wish.

We wish to use the vows on
    page 6
    page 29
    page 30
    with / without 'obey'

Who is going to make the first vow?

Bride / Groom

The Giving of Rings

There are two alternative prayers of blessing of the rings – on page 7 and page 30.

We would like the blessing on page 7 / 30

Will you be using one ring, or exchanging rings?

We will be using one / two rings

Do you wish to say the words together or separately, and if the latter, who goes first?

Together
separately (bride / groom)

The Blessing of the Marriage

There are several forms of Blessing, on page 9 and pages 31–2. Which one do you want to use? You can use the one on page 32 on its own, or add it to one of the others. There are also three other forms which you can choose instead, if you prefer. They are in the *Additional Prayers* leaflet you have in your folder.

We would like to use
   page 9
   page 31
   page 32
   alone / as well
   other form

The Registration of the Marriage

If you are signing, as most people do, in church (chancel or Lady chapel), it takes place at this point. If you use the vestry, it happens right at the end of the service. You each need to choose a witness to sign.

We will sign in church
chancel / Lady chapel
We will sign in the vestry

What music do you want while we are signing the registers? It can be organ music, other live music, or a tape or CD.

Music

What hymn will you sing at this point?

Hymn

The Prayers

A variety of forms is provided, which you can find in the *Additional Prayers* leaflet in the folder, or you can write your own – in which case, discuss with the vicar whether you can have what you have written. Some of the forms cover all four topics suggested within one prayer.

Others are single-topic prayers. There is no 'right' number to use. Have what is right for you.

We want the following

Which version of the Lord's Prayer?

Thee and thy / You and your

What hymn will you sing at this point?

Hymn

The Dismissal

What music will you use while you walk out of church?

Music

Thanksgiving for Marriage: An Outline Order

Introduction

- Welcome

- Prayer of Preparation

- Preface

- Readings

- Psalms, Songs or Hymns

- Sermon

Renewal of Vows

- The couple(s) are invited to renew their marriage vows in a suitable form.

- A ring or rings may be blessed.

- Prayers are offered, including prayers of thanksgiving and blessing.

A sample version of how this might work out is to be found in Common Worship: Pastoral Services, *pages 186–93.*

Readings

My beloved speaks and says to me:
'Arise, my love, my fair one,
and come away;
for now the winter is past,
the rain is over and gone.
The flowers appear on the earth;
the time of singing has come,
and the voice of the turtle dove
is heard in our land.
The fig tree puts forth its figs,
and the vines are in blossom;
they give forth fragrance.
Arise, my love, my fair one,
and come away.'

Set me as a seal upon your heart,
as a seal upon your arm;
for love is strong as death,
passion fierce as the grave.
Its flashes are flashes of fire,
a raging flame.
Many waters cannot quench love,
neither can floods drown it.
If one offered for love
all the wealth of one's house,
it would be utterly scorned.

Song of Solomon 2.10-13; 8.6,7

When the parents had gone out and shut the door of the room, Tobias got out of bed and said to Sarah, 'Sister, get up, and let us pray and implore our Lord that he grant us mercy and safety.' So she got up, and they began to pray and implore that they might be kept safe. Tobias began by saying,
 'Blessed are you, O God of our ancestors,
and blessed is your name in all generations for ever.
Let the heavens and the whole creation bless you for ever.
You made Adam, and for him you made his wife Eve
as a helper and support.
From the two of them the human race has sprung.
You said, "It is not good that the man should be alone;
let us make a helper for him like himself."
I now am taking this kinswoman of mine,
not because of lust,
but with sincerity.
Grant that she and I may find mercy
and that we may grow old together.'
And they both said, 'Amen, amen.'

Tobit 8.4-8

Questions for a reunion course

- Something that has been a surprise – why was that?

- Something that has been better than you expected – why was that?

- Something that has been a disappointment – why was that?

- Take stock of how these three things have changed and developed. How are things different between you from before you were married? Why have they changed? Are those changes all good? If not, what can you do about it?

Companionship and Friendship

Sex

Children

RESOURCE SHEET  21

Scripted version of the sessions for a one-day course

If you are using this script, please also read the chapter called 'Practical matters' and the notes on preparation, materials and timings included in 'A one-day course', both in the main part of the book.

A one-day course

The questions for the couples can be found at Resource sheet 1.

Introduction

(10–15 minutes – will depend on the number of participants)

It is good to welcome you to this day exploring marriage. I wonder if you know that poem by the American humourist Ogden Nash which ends:

> *That is why marriage is so much more interesting than divorce,*
> *Because it's the only known example of the happy meeting of*
> *the immovable object and the irresistible force.*
> *So I hope husbands and wives will continue to debate and*
> *combat over everything debatable and combatable,*
> *Because I believe a little incompatibility is the spice of life,*
> *particularly if he has income and she is pattable.*

(You may prefer to substitute some other favourite light-hearted poem or anecdote to break the ice.)

The Group Contract:

- Confidentiality
- We shall be mostly talking privately in pairs, but there is *no obligation* to share anything with the wider group.
- When we work together, everyone has the right to say 'Pass'.
- Timekeeping: we shall be living with frustration – you will want to have had more time on some things, but we have to get through a lot. You can always go on talking at home!

Introductions

Please would each couple give their names and say:

- How long you have known each other
- How long you have been living together (if they have been) and
- When you are getting married.

(Leader(s) should also introduce themselves, using the same format as far as possible. If the leader(s) work(s) through this process first it will form a model for others to follow and give the first couple time to think.)

How are you feeling?

Please would each of you share one word about your feelings about this course. If someone uses your word before you do, fine – just repeat it. It will be interesting to see what feelings are shared. *(List the words on a flip chart or OHP and make a brief comment on range and/or commonality of the feelings expressed.)*

Doing something like this is a worthwhile investment of time. Unless people have an opportunity to stand back and think about what they are doing, they can find their energies are easily diverted onto secondary issues, rather than the relationship itself. The way we will be working some of the time – giving each other one-to-one space to talk and think – is a model for how you can interact throughout your lives together.

Why this one?

(20 minutes)

In groups of four if possible, but otherwise in pairs (**10 minutes**)

Spend a couple of minutes each saying why, out of all humanity, you have chosen this one to marry. What is it about him or her that makes you want to do that? See how much you can embarrass each other!

Note that there will be no reporting back on this exercise, so you only have to say something in front of two other people who are in the same boat.

In the whole group (**10 minutes**)

Did you find the reasons were the same? Similar? Or quite different?

That is why no one can advise anyone else on how to be married. We all have different needs, expectations and fears. Many of you will have watched *The Good Life*. Tom and Barbara are happily married, and so are Margot and Gerry; but none of them could possibly be married to their 'opposite number' in the other house.

You are already involved in an adventure of getting to know another person better than anyone else in the world – and maybe discovering things about yourself as well.

Past, present and future

(45 minutes – in 3 × 15-minute segments)

The past

Introduction (5 minutes)

For the next 45 minutes I want to help you explore three vital times – the past, the present and the future. It would seem logical to start with the past.

Let's just go round the group again, and this time I would like each of you to tell us something about yourself that your partner (as far as you are aware) doesn't know. It may be something that happened to you when you were very small, or it may be something that happened yesterday. It doesn't have to be anything very important – even what you had for lunch, if you can't think of anything else!

(Go round the group.)

Now, that probably wasn't very difficult – because, however well you know each other, you simply can't yet have shared everything that has ever happened to you. There hasn't been time. We think we know each other well, but actually we don't know each other as well as we think. Lots of things get talked about only when something happens to trigger a memory. Counsellors find that sometimes things are triggered for someone when their child reaches a particular age, and they suddenly start remembering for themselves what it was like to be changing school, or whatever. Most of the things we have not shared are simply things forgotten for the time being. But sometimes they are painful memories that we have pushed to the back of our minds because we can't cope with them. It may be that our partner is the first person we dare share some bad memories with. That is part of the intimacy, the closeness of marriage.

We all bring to marriage images of what it is like to be a husband or a wife. We get those primarily from the people who brought us up. That could be simply a mum and dad, or it may be that we didn't have both, in which case our pictures will be fantasies based on friends who had both. Perhaps we have been part of more than one marriage, and we have a step-parent to inform our ideas. The images will also be coloured by other marriages we have seen – grandparents, or aunts and uncles.

What I would like you to do as couples is to spend about ten minutes sharing with each other good and bad things that come from your experience in the past. What are the things about the marriages you have been part of as children which you would want to be the same in your marriage, and what are the things you would want to be different? You might like to think about whether your ideas about those things are the same as your partner's, or different. There is no reporting back – this is your private discussion.

Work in pairs **(10 minutes)**

The future

Introduction and drawing (5 minutes)

We started, logically, with the past, so let's go on, illogically, to the future. The marriage industry thrives on dreams. There is an old joke about the dreams that brides have about their wedding day. They dream about waking down the aisle to the altar and singing a hymn. So they have those three words in their mind: I'll – alter – him!

Now, if there is one thing I cannot do it is to draw – no, not quite true, I can't dance either! So if I now ask you to do some drawing, I want to speak to people like me and say that this doesn't have to be a work of art for others to admire. What I would like you to do – on your own, first of all – is to draw a picture, or maybe some symbols, which represent what you dream your married life will be like in, say, ten years' time. You may want to draw a real picture, or maybe just symbols – like £ signs to indicate that you expect to have made your fortune! Just give yourselves two or three minutes to draw something which is 'Us in ten years' time' (*Resource sheet 2*).

Drawing

Now, would you go off with your partner and talk about your pictures for five minutes. I will ask you then, if you are willing, when we come back together to share whether or not your dreams turned out to be exactly the same.

Sharing in pairs **(5 minutes)**

Whole group sharing **(5 minutes)**

Are the dreams the same? How does that make you feel?

The present

Introduction (7 minutes)

The reason we are coming to the present last of all is because there is a sense in which the present is the melting pot in which your history and your dreams meet. Every day you are using the past and the future to create this present moment. I am going to ask you to go off in pairs again in a moment, but I wonder if first of all we could spend a minute or two sharing together what it feels like to be at this stage – when the wedding is booked, and the plans are being made. What are the best and the worst things about this stage in your history as a couple?

Sharing (on flip chart or OHP if desired)

Before we break for coffee, I would like you to do some private sharing about what difference getting married is going to make to you. If you are not living together, there will be some pretty basic changes, but it is worth spelling these out. But if you are already together, in a sense the question is even more important. Do you expect getting married to make a difference to you, or not? If so, what difference will it make? If not, why not? This is not an easy thing to tease out. If you say 'No', then you may want to explain why you *do* want to get married. If you say 'Yes', then what does that say about the development of your relationship, and how it might move on? There is no reporting back. We'll tell you when coffee is ready.

Sharing in pairs **(8 minutes)**

Coffee break **(15 minutes)**

Five topics

Introduction (3 minutes)

Between now and lunch, we are going to begin to open up just five topics which are pretty important. The first three are reasons given in the wedding service for getting married, and the other two are things that underlie lots of other topics that you might want to talk about in detail at another time – and I will explain how you might do that just before lunch.

Let me read you the reasons as they come in *Common Worship*. They are the same in the other orders of service that are still legal, although they come in a different order. But I don't think the order is particularly important.

The gift of marriage brings husband and wife together
in the delight and tenderness of sexual union
and joyful commitment to the end of their lives.
It is given as the foundation of family life
in which children are [born and] nurtured
and in which each member of the family,
in good times and in bad,
may find strength, companionship and comfort,
and grow to maturity in love.

Sex

Introduction (5 minutes)

If we take them in the order they come in. Sex is the first – and the service is daring enough to use the word 'sexual'. I am glad about that. There has been a myth around for far too long that God and sex don't mix, and you shouldn't mention things like that in front of the vicar. As you know, there are three sexes: men, women and clergy. Well, I have news for you: that is rubbish. You only have to take a step back to see what nonsense it is. If we believe that God made us, he made us as sexual beings, or at least allowed us to develop into sexual beings. We could still be splitting like an amoeba, but it wouldn't be much fun. Sex is God's gift to us and, far from being naughty, it is something holy and wonderful and to be celebrated. But like any other skill, although it is the most natural thing in the world, it has to be learned, and your task is to be each other's teacher. Men don't know a thing about being women, and women don't know a thing about being men, but they sometimes like to pretend they do. However good any sex education we had was – and the chances are it wasn't all that good – we still have to learn a lot from each other, and go on learning, because how we like to express love physically will change as the years go by. Our attitudes may well be coloured by our upbringings. I wonder how much you have shared those with each other. It can raise issues. A person from a prudish kind of home may find living with a partner who comes from a home where nudity and openness about sex is normal quite a threat. I have to say, surprisingly often it is the men who are more threatened than the women! Many couples take quite a long time to settle down sexually – if that is the case for you, just be assured that is very normal. But if you are really having problems, do look for some help sooner rather than later. Why miss out on something that God intends to be so good?

Now I *could* ask you to join in a general discussion about that – but one of the important things about sex is that it is intimate and private. So I am going to ask you to go with your partner again and just share a little about one question: 'What does sex add to your whole relationship?' You have about seven minutes. Some of you might think that is an appropriate time!

Sharing in pairs **(7 minutes)**

Children

Introduction (5 minutes)

I guess that in your 'dream' picture some of you may well have included the number of children you expect to have in ten years' time. You may have had the same number in your two pictures; but maybe not. It is startling to find the occasional couple who are about to get married who have never talked about whether they want children; or how many; or when. It is a basic sort of issue to tackle. There are huge questions around all this in our particular day and age. The average age for having children has gone up markedly – and there are obvious economic and career reasons for that. It's worth reflecting on how the shape of marriage has changed from what it was a hundred years ago. In those days people had their children right away, because there was really no adequate and safe contraception. They had more children, for the same reason, and very often some of those children died. By the time they had stopped having and bringing up children, probably one of the partners would die. So they had very little time just as a couple together. Compare that with now, when we have acres of time as a couple, either before we have our two children or less (which is now is the average, not the 2.4 everyone talks about), or after the children have left home, or both. The child-bearing and raising years are just a small fraction of our time. We are free to choose when those years will be. There are big questions about whether to answer that in a way that benefits ourselves or the children.

Well, you have your dream. I want to be a bit negative, and ask you to think about a nightmare. I wonder if you know how many couples get sufficiently worried that they can't conceive a child that they go to the doctor? It is roughly one in six (happily, most of them not having a real problem). But there genuinely is a problem at the moment, and everything from the ozone layer down has been blamed. So I think it is very useful to have faced up to 'What would we feel?' 'What would we do?' if that applied to us. Hopefully it won't. Five out of six couples have no problem. But it is much easier to talk about it when it isn't the emotional issue it would then be. You can always change your mind – but your discussion will have given you a starting point. There are so many choices (and thank God that we have IVF and the like), but every choice is another complication; another joint decision that has to be made.

So, as couples again, would you take ten minutes to talk about 'How you would feel if you had difficulty conceiving' – and what would you want to do? If you are a couple who don't want to have children (or to have any more children), you might like instead to talk about what you would do if you found you *had* conceived. Again, there will no reporting back.

Sharing in pairs **(10 minutes)**

Companionship

Introduction (5 minutes)

The third reason in the service we will look at is what we might call companionship, or friendship. Most couples meet as friends first of all, before they fall in love. For some, that means that friendship gets pushed into second place. Being lovers is the task of the moment. But at the end of the day, friendship is the longest lasting of all these three. Sex will, I hope, still be important when you are 80; but it will be less important than now. If you have children, they will hopefully have left home by then. But you might be leaning on each other literally, as well as metaphorically. Being friends is a basic requirement for a good marriage.

Many people include in their wedding service those famous words from Kahlil Gibran's *The Prophet*:

> *And stand together, yet not too near together,*
> *For the pillars of the temple stand apart*
> *And the oak tree and the cypress grow not in each other's shadow.*

There is great wisdom in that. How we spend time – together and apart; with friends as well as with each other – is something we all have to negotiate. Just talk to someone other than your partner for a minute or two about this sort of thing, and how you handle togetherness and apartness in your relationship, and then let's have a general discussion about it.

General discussion **(10 minutes)**

Communication

Introduction (2 minutes)

One of the basic skills we all need is good communication. Certainly the most common thing people say when they go for marriage counselling is that communications have broken down. There are two parts to that, aren't there? One is talking – because if you don't talk to each other, how can you know what the other one thinks and feels? Silence can be wonderful, when it is relaxed companionable silence – we don't need to talk all the time, because it is nice just 'to be'. Silence can also be awful – when it is awkward and a sign of tension.

But the second skill is listening. If people don't listen, it doesn't matter how much someone talks. In these exercises we are about to do, we will all stay in this room, although we will be working in pairs, because I won't be asking you to share anything private. In a moment I am going to get you to do some talking and listening. But just to remind you that words are not the only way of communicating, could you just take your intended's hand, and then the two of you take it in turns to express an emotion by the way you hold it. Close your eyes; otherwise you will also be using facial expressions, which is another important way of communicating.

Hand messages **(2 minutes)**

Now let's move towards lunch with a bit of listening and talking. First of all, find someone other than your partner. Just talk to that person for a minute, non-stop, about what you did yesterday. Both of you do it *at the same time* – just talk *at* each other without listening to the other. It's up to you to keep going.

Simultaneous talk **(1 minute)**

How did that feel? **(2 minutes)**

Now work with your proper partner. Would one person in each couple first of all tell a story – perhaps about something that happened to you when the other person wasn't there. You have just two minutes. Would the other person please do their very best to ignore the person speaking. Look the other way; fiddle with your watch; whatever you like – but don't pay any attention.

Ignored talk **(2 minutes)**

Now what did that feel like? **(2 minutes)**

Now could you reverse roles, so the 'rude' one becomes the storyteller. You have two minutes. But this time the listener should pay full attention.

Careful listening **(2 minutes)**

Now would the listener please recount that story. You have one minute. This is about total recall. But could you now also say what *emotions* were coming over to you. The storyteller should think what it felt like to be listened to, and whether you were heard accurately.

Recall **(1 minute)**

All those things can and do happen in relationships. People talk at each other without listening. They ignore each other. And sometimes they listen with full attention: sometimes to the facts, and sometimes also to the emotions; to what isn't being said in words. And we can all improve our listening and talking skills. The Children's Society once ran a very perceptive campaign under the slogan 'This child needs a good listening to.'

Conflict

Introduction (2 minutes)

You have a piece of paper with four rough graphs (*Resource sheet 3*). The first three are unrealistic maps of how a marriage will be. The first represents ever-increasing bliss. The second represents ever-increasing misery. The third represents no change at all – everything just as it is, for ever. If you think that any of those is how your relationships are, then you have a problem.

The last one is the reality. There will be ups and downs in everyone's relationships, but the vital thing is how we handle them.

What I would like you to have a go at is plotting individually, on the back of that sheet, a graph of how you as an individual see your relationship so far. Hopefully there haven't been any major 'downs', but there will almost certainly have been little blips: perhaps stresses caused from outside when a house purchase fell through, or when there was a bereavement.

Graph plotting (3 minutes)

Now go off with your partner and compare notes and talk about what you have drawn, and whether you have both seen the ups and downs in the same way.

Then, lastly, have a think about the skills you have that help you cope with the less good moments, the irritations and crossed wires that happen. How do you get through those? How do you make up? I tend to think of it in terms of a first-aid box. I hope you have one, and that you know what plasters and bandages are in it. What are the equivalent first-aid things that help bandage your relationship when it gets a bruise? It may be being good at listening; at giving each other space; having a sense of humour – I guess you will come up with quite a number. You have got ten minutes for those two tasks: reflecting on your graphs and thinking about your first-aid box; you can divide the time as you prefer.

Sharing in pairs **(10 minutes)**

Pre-lunch summary

Introduction (3 minutes)

I have picked up just five topics, and we have really only scratched the surface of those. I am sure we could have spent all morning on just one. We could equally well have talked about how you get on with the wider family; how you see your own roles; how you cope with money – the list is endless. However, when we finish today you are going to get a copy of a book called *Growing Together*, which was written by a clergyman with a great deal of experience of working with couples: not only in his parish, but as a marriage counsellor. The book is designed for couples to use on their own, to help them deepen their understanding of each other. We have used this morning about eight of the questions that are in the book – and there are over 150 altogether for you to talk about together, if you want. It also has some stories of real people, who might provoke some discussion as well. Each chapter is structured around those three topics we started with – Past, Present and Future. So it will, I hope, enable you to do what it says on the tin: *Grow Together*.

After lunch we are going to pick up one other topic from it, and also look at some practical issues about the wedding day, rather than the state of being married. But we have just a few minutes before lunch, if anyone wants to ask any questions, or raise anything that has come out of what we have done so far.

Questions and comments (**Up to 12 minutes, unless there has been time slippage earlier!**)

Lunch break (**45 minutes**)

Faith

Introduction (1 minute)

In about 15 minutes, and for the rest of our time together, we are going to turn our attention a bit more to the wedding ceremony. But first of all I want to use the fact that you have decided to get married in church to open up questions of faith. You might all be regular worshippers, or you might never have set foot in the church, but somehow or other you have all come to the decision that a church wedding is what you want. What I would like you to do for a minute or two is to write on a piece of paper *your* reason for getting married in church: not you as a couple; not your partner's reason; but *your own*. I am going to mix them up then, so we don't know who has said what, and we will see what sort of reasons there are. Please be ruthlessly honest – if the reason is to keep your parents quiet, or whatever, then say so!

Individual work (**2 minutes**)

Shared results (on flipchart or OHP if desired) (**3 minutes**)

You all come with an individual faith journey. It may be a long one, or very short one. People often say 'I'm not very religious'. Well, we are all believers or not believers – in others words, we all have a religious position that we are in at this moment. That may change. Changes like that can be a challenge in a marriage, if suddenly someone who has not been very religious gets religion big-time; or for that matter, if someone who has been very religious loses their faith. Our faith journeys are personal, but they have an effect on our partner. Apart from getting married in church, there will be other faith decisions that you will make. If you have children, for example, will you have them baptized?

So let's just have one last short session in pairs. Sometimes people think it is strange that people who don't usually go to church want to have their wedding there. Ask them to imagine they are being interviewed for a TV programme by someone who thinks like that. What are the things they would want to say in reply. No reporting back – their private discussion for eight minutes.

Sharing in pairs (**8 minutes**)

Making decisions about the wedding

(50 minutes)

It is your day – and they are your choices. Personalize as much as you can. You may well want to involve other people in what happens. You will, though, need to check with the vicar the various things you would like to do.

(Resource sheet 17 is a work sheet that can be used as it is or adapted to suit local usage.)

Order of service

Strictly speaking, there are three orders of service that are legal: the 1662 Book of Common Prayer, the 1928 Prayer Book (Series 1) and *Common Worship* (2000). In practice *Common Worship* probably has everything you might want, including a form of wedding with Holy Communion, which is an option any of you who are regular communicants might want to consider. It doesn't have to add a lot of time to the service.

Choreography

- Who walks in with whom
- Where people stand or sit
- 'Giving away' or alternatives
- Where you sign the registers
- Other practical issues

Hymns

- There is space in the service for four, but you don't have to have that many.
- The most important thing is that people should know the hymns you choose. It's embarrassing for the vicar to have to sing a solo!
- Some hymns fit better in one place than another. So, for example, a hymn about vows goes well at the point you are about to make them; or a hymn which is a prayer just before the prayers. It is also generally best to go out on the most joyous note.
- Do check that the tune the organist has in mind is the same as the tune you are expecting. Some popular hymns, such as 'Love divine' and 'At the name of Jesus', have more than one well-known tune.
- Copyright issues.
- Start thinking now! People pick up ideas when they go to church on Sundays, or to other people's weddings.

Readings

- Who? This is a good time to involve other people, but do emphasize that any readers will need to practise. In particular, some readings can contain tricky names: Balaam, for instance.
- What? At least one of the readings must come from the Bible. There are 26 suggestions in *Common Worship*, but you can also choose others if you wish.
- Take care to read all of these, and then cut them down to a short list. Why do the readings on the short list speak to you?
- Let me share with you two readings that, after the 1 Corinthians reading, I find are being chosen very often these days. The first is from the Song of Solomon (sometimes called 'the Song of Songs'). It is a really quite erotic poem, which talks about God's love in terms of human passion. This reading doesn't include the parts about the beloved's breasts being like twin fawns, or clusters of grapes, or the man's legs being like alabaster columns set upon bases of gold. This is the bit that it does use. You need to think of a woman hiding behind the lattice window of a Middle Eastern house, with the lover whispering through the window.

(Incidentally, it says in another place that he has arrived there bounding like a young gazelle across the desert!) This is how it goes:

- [Read Song of Solomon 2.10-13; 8.6-7.]
- The second is from the Apocrypha – the books from Old Testament times that were left out of some versions of the Bible. This one is from the book of Tobit.
- [Read Tobit 8.4-8.]
- The context of that one is rather fun too, but you wouldn't guess it from the bit we heard. The couple are praying before their first night together. But Sarah has been previously given in marriage to seven other men. Unfortunately, before the marriage was consummated, they were all killed by a demon called Asmodeus. Now, people were as sceptical about the reality of demons then as they are today, and they quite reasonably said it was Sarah who had killed them off. If you think this story is bizarre, I have to say 'You ain't heard nothin' yet!' Tobias is very smitten with Sarah, but he has a meeting with the Archangel Raphael, and after another curious incident when a huge fish tries to swallow Tobias's foot when he washes it in the Tigris, he is told by the angel to catch the fish and eat the flesh, but to keep the gall, heart and liver, because they are useful in dealing with demons. So, come his first night with Sarah, when they are obviously both on edge that he might be Victim Number Eight, he takes the precaution of burning these bits of old fish guts as a way of dealing with Asmodeus – which works. Apparently it smells so bad he takes off to Upper Egypt, where Raphael deals with him once and for all.
- Make sure that you have the right translation – the one you want the passage read from – and that the reader knows which one will be on the lectern at the service.
- Non-biblical readings are very personal and entirely optional. The most important thing is that what you choose means something to you. All of these need to be OK'd with the vicar. Some brave brides and grooms have written something themselves.

Prayers

- Again, a time when you can make the service very much your own.
- There is one set of prayers in the main text of the service, but lots of others in *Common Worship: Pastoral Services*. The idea generally is that you choose either one of the longer prayers (with the 'response' style) or one from each of the sections of short ones.
- Prayers from elsewhere can also be used.
- Or you can write your own.

Music

- Music sets the tone and is an important part of the service. There are three basic times when music is used:
    - Entry
    - During the signing of the Registers – probably 5–7 minutes
    - Exit.

- The organ is the usual instrument. Do, though, make sure that the music you choose suits both the building and the organ. People can be led astray by listening to discs. And can the organist play it?
- Recordings can be used, if there is a playing system available. It may be advisable to burn a track on a disk, rather than risk the wrong music being played by mistake.
- Is live music from your friends or family an option for any of you?

Oddments

- Banns
- Fees
- Confetti
- Photos and/or videos
- Other practical issues

Ending

(10 minutes)

- Thank you for coming!
- Are there any questions?
- If any personal issues have been raised for anyone by any of today's sessions, please do feel free to speak to me afterwards, and I will do my best to help, or suggest other places where help may be available.
- Give out the books.
- Pray the following prayer to end the day.

> There are so many choices:
>> venues and menus,
>> dresses and tresses,
>> shades and bridesmaids,
>> cars and guitars,
>> houses and blouses,
>> speeches and preachers;
> It is so easy to over-spend, to lose all sense of proportion.
> Help us to plan not only for the day, but for the rest of our life.
> Help us to choose the best things:
>> faith
>> hope
>> love.

(Andrew Body, from *Pocket Prayers for Marriage*)

Scripted version of the sessions for a six- plus one-week course

If you are using these scripts, please also read the chapter called 'Practical matters' and the practical notes on preparation, materials and timings in the main part of the book.

Week 1: Introductions; past, present and future

Introduction
(20 minutes – will depend on the number of participants)

It's good to welcome you to this course exploring marriage. I wonder if you know that poem by the American humourist Ogden Nash that ends:

> *That is why marriage is so much more interesting than divorce,*
> *Because it's the only known example of the happy meeting of*
> *the immovable object and the irresistible force.*
> *So I hope husbands and wives will continue to debate and*
> *combat over everything debatable and combatable,*
> *Because I believe a little incompatibility is the spice of life,*
> *particularly if he has income and she is pattable.*

(You may prefer to substitute some other favourite light-hearted poem or anecdote to break the ice.)

The Group Contract

- Confidentiality
- The course is conducted mostly through talking privately in pairs, but there is *no obligation* to share anything at all with the wider group.
- When we work together, everyone has the right to say 'Pass'.
- Timekeeping: you will all be living with frustration in this connection. You will want to have had more time on some things, but we do have to get through a lot. You can always go on talking at home!

Introductions

Please would each couple give their names and say:

- How long you have known each other
- How long you have been living together (if they have been) and
- When you are getting married.

(Leader(s) should also introduce themselves, using the same format as far as possible. If the leader(s) work(s) through this process first, it will form a model for others to follow and give the first couple time to think.)

How are you feeling?

Please would each of you share one word about your feelings about this course. If someone uses your word, fine – just repeat it. It will be interesting to see what feelings are shared. *(List on flip chart or OHP, following up with brief comment on range and/or commonality of the feelings expressed.)*

Doing something like this course is a worthwhile investment of time. Unless people have an opportunity to stand back and think about what they are doing, they can find their energies are easily diverted onto secondary issues, rather than the relationship itself. The way we will be working some of the time – giving each other one-to-one space to talk and think – is a model for how you can interact throughout your lives together.

Introduction to the course

- ■   List some of the topics to be covered, now and in future sessions.
- ■   Explain the practical details of running the sessions.
- ■   Mention the book *Growing Together*, to be given either tonight or at the end of the course.

The past

Introduction (5 minutes)

For the rest of this evening I want us explore three vital times – the past, the present and the future. It would seem logical to start with the past.

Let's just go round the group again, and this time I would like each of you to tell us something about yourself that your partner (as far as you are aware) doesn't know. It may be something that happened to you when you were very small; or it may be something that happened yesterday. It doesn't have to be anything very important – even what you had for lunch, if you can't think of anything else!

(Contributions from participants.)

Now that probably wasn't very difficult – because, however well you know each other, you simply can't yet have shared everything that has ever happened to you. There hasn't been time. We think we know each other well, but actually we don't know each other as well as we think. Lots of things get talked about only when something happens to trigger a memory. Counsellors find that sometimes memories are triggered for someone when their child reaches a particular age, and they suddenly start remembering for themselves what it was like to be changing schools, or whatever. Most of the things we have not shared are simply things forgotten for the time being. But sometimes they are painful memories that we have pushed to the back of our minds because we can't cope with them. It may be that our partner is the first person we dare share some bad memories with. That is part of the intimacy, the closeness of marriage.

(Tell or read the story of Paula and Graham (Growing Together, *p. 16).)*

We all bring to marriage images of what it is like to be a husband or a wife. We get those primarily from the people who brought us up. That could be simply a mum and dad; or it may be that we didn't have both, in which case, our images will be fantasies, based perhaps on friends who had both. It may be that as we grew up we have been part of more than one marriage, and we have a step-parent to inform our ideas. The images will also be coloured by other marriages we have seen – grandparents, or aunts and uncles.

What I would like you to do as couples is to spend about 15 minutes sharing with each other good and bad things that come from your experience in the past. What are the things about the marriages you have been part of as children which you would want to be the same in your marriage? What things would you want to be different? You might like to think about whether your ideas about these things are the same as your partner's, or different. There is no reporting back after this – this is your private discussion.

Work in pairs **(15 minutes)**

The future

Introduction and drawing (15 minutes)

We started, logically, with the past, so let's go on, illogically, to the future. The marriage industry thrives on dreams. There is an old joke about the dreams that brides have about their wedding day. They dream about walking down the aisle to the altar and singing a hymn. So they have those three words in their mind: I'll – alter – him!

Now if there is one thing I cannot do it is to draw – no, not quite true, I can't dance either! So if I now ask you to do some drawing, I want to speak to people like me and say that this doesn't have to be a work of art for others to admire. What I would like you to do, on your own first of all, is to draw a picture that represents what you dream your married life will be like in, say, ten years' time. You might want to draw a real picture, or maybe symbols – like £ signs to indicate that you expect to have made your fortune. Just give yourselves two or three minutes to draw something that is 'Us in ten years' time'.

Drawing **(2 minutes)**

Now would you go off with your partner and talk about your pictures for five minutes. I will ask you, if you are willing, when we come back together to share whether your dreams are exactly the same.

Sharing in pairs **(8 minutes)**

Whole group sharing **(5 minutes)**

Were both dreams the same? And how does that make you feel?

The present

Introduction (10 minutes)

The reason we are coming to the present last of all is because there is a sense in which the present is the melting pot in which your history and your dreams meet. Every day you are using the past and the future to create this moment. I am going to ask you to go off in pairs again in a moment, but I wonder if, first of all, we could spend a minute or two sharing together what it feels like to be at this stage, when the wedding is booked, and the plans are being made. What are the best and worst things about this stage in your history as a couple?

Sharing (*using flip chart or OHP if desired*).

(*Talk about pressures from family and/or wedding industry.*)

Now, I would like you to do some private sharing about what difference getting married is going to make to you. If you are not living together, there will be some pretty basic changes, but it is worth spelling these out. But if you are already together, in a sense the question is even more important. Do you expect getting married to make a difference to you, or not? If so, what difference will it make? If not, why not? It's not an easy thing to tease out. If you say 'No', then you have to ask yourselves 'Why bother, then?' If you say 'Yes', then what is that saying about the development of your relationship, and how it might move on? There is no reporting back. We'll tell you when coffee is ready.

Sharing in pairs (**10 minutes**)

If timings have gone well, there should be about ten minutes left. If not, you will need to edit or omit all or part of this final section.

Ending
(10 minutes)

On the piece of paper provided (*Resource sheet 4*) you will find two columns. One has an exclamation mark on it, the other a question mark. Under the exclamation mark would you please jot down, *individually*, any new thought that has occurred to you this evening. It doesn't have to be something profound! And under the question mark, put down anything that has raised questions you want to pursue further. There will be an opportunity at the beginning of the next session, if you want it, to share anything that has come out of this evening – but there will be no pressure to say anything if you prefer not to.

Individual responses (2 minutes)

We will stay together in this room, but now, in pairs, but with someone *other* than your partner, just take two minutes to share any 'exclamation mark' thoughts which have come to you as a result of this evening.

Sharing in pairs (2 minutes)

And then, with your *real* partner, share any 'question mark' areas which have come up this evening and which you would like to explore further with each other.

Sharing as couples (2 minutes)

It may be that this evening has raised some personal issues for you that you didn't want to share with the group, or even with each other. Do feel free to speak to me if you want some time to talk anything through individually.

Lastly, let's take a minute or two in silence to reflect on all that has been said, both together and privately. I will then offer all those thoughts to God in a short prayer to close.

Week 2: Reasons for getting married

Introduction
(20 minutes)

Welcome back. I hope that if you had things you wanted to discuss further with each other, you have found time to do it. Does anyone want to comment on things they have discussed?

There is *no obligation* to do so, but it would be good, if you want to, to share a word or two about anything with each other.

Feedback (**3 minutes**)

Tonight we are going to talk about the reasons for getting married. The most important reasons are the ones you have, and we will start off by exploring those.

Why this one?

(15 minutes)

EITHER:

In groups of four (**10 minutes**)

With one other couple, form into a group of four people. Spend a couple of minutes each saying why – out of all humanity – you have chosen this person to marry. What is it about him or her that makes you want to do that? See how much you can embarrass each other! Do note that there will be no reporting back, so you only have to speak in front of two other people who are in the same boat.

In the whole group (**5 minutes**)

Did you find the reasons were the same? Similar? Or quite different?

OR:

Write on a piece of paper, anonymously, three reasons why – out of all humanity – you have chosen this person to marry. What is it about him or her that makes you want to do that? The reasons can be as light-hearted as 'is the only person who really understands me' or as serious as 'has the sexiest kneecaps I have ever seen'. If you avoid saying 'he' or 'she', this will make it more fun. I will mix up the papers before we read them out.

Individual work (**2 minutes**), followed by sharing and listing on flip chart or OHP (**5 minutes**)

So these are the reasons – I wonder how many of you recognize your partner's reasons?

Are the reasons the same? Similar? Or quite different?

General discussion (**8 minutes**)

Introduction to the Preface

(5 minutes)

There are many different reasons for getting married. That is why no one can advise anyone else on how to be married. We all have different needs, expectations and fears. Many of you will have watched *The Good Life*. Tom and Barbara are happily married, and so are Margot and Gerry; but none of them could possibly be married to their 'opposite number' in the other house.

But there are probably also some things in common. In the wedding service, there is a section towards the beginning, called 'The Preface', that among other things sets out three reasons for marriage. In essence, these are 'children, sex and companionship'. How those reasons have been expressed, and the order in which they are listed, has varied through the ages. This is how it reads in *Common Worship*:

The gift of marriage brings husband and wife together
in the delight and tenderness of sexual union
and joyful commitment to the end of their lives.
It is given as the foundation of family life
in which children are [born and] nurtured
and in which each member of the family,
in good times and in bad,
may find strength, companionship and comfort,
and grow to maturity in love.

(If time allows, you may also like to read equivalent parts of the Alternative Preface from Common Worship, *and that from* The Book of Common Prayer.*)*

Think of those three reasons as the legs of a three-legged stool. That is enough to give you solid support. It may be that sometimes one leg is shorter than the others, but as long as you have all three legs on the stool, you won't fall down. For the rest of this evening, we are going to explore those three reasons, and since *Growing Together* works through topics in alphabetical order, we will do the same.

Children
(20 minutes)

I guess that, in your 'dream' picture you made last week, some of you may well have put the number of children you expect to have in ten years' time. Some of you may have had the same number in your two pictures; some not. It is startling to find the occasional couple about to get married who have never talked about whether they want children; or how many; or when. It is a basic sort of issue to tackle. There are huge questions around all this in our particular day and age. The average age for having children has gone up markedly. There are obvious economic and career reasons for that. It's worth reflecting, too, on how the shape of marriage has changed from what it was a hundred years ago. In those days people had their children right away, because there was really no adequate and safe contraception. They had more children for the same reason, and very often some of their children died. By the time they stopped having and bringing up children, probably one of the partners would die too. So they had very little time as just a couple. Compare that with now, when we have acres of time as a couple, either before we have our two children or less – which is now is the average, not the 2.4 everyone talks about – or after the children have left home, or both. The child-bearing and raising years are just a small fraction of our time. We are free to choose when those years will be. There are big questions about whether we answer that in a way that is for the benefit of ourselves, or the children.

As a group, let's just jot down the factors which help people decide how many children they want, and when.

List factors on flip chart or OHP, and follow up with general discussion. **(5 minutes)**

Well, you have your dream.

Now, I want to be a bit negative and ask you to think about a nightmare. I wonder if you know how many couples get sufficiently worried that they can't conceive a child that they go to the doctor? It is roughly one in six (happily, most of them not having a real problem). But there genuinely is a problem at the moment, and everything from the ozone layer down has been blamed for it. So I think it is very useful to have faced up to 'What would we feel?' and

'What would we do?' if that applied to us. Hopefully it won't – five couples out of six have no problem. But it is much easier to talk about it when it isn't the emotional issue it would then be. You can always change your mind – but your discussion will have given you a starting point. There are so many choices (and thank God that we have IVF and the like), but every choice is another complication; another joint decision that has to be made.

So, as couples again, would you take ten minutes to talk about 'How you would feel if you had difficulty conceiving', and what you would want to do. If you are a couple who doesn't want to have children (or to have any more children), you might like instead to talk about what you would do if you found you *had* conceived. Again, there will be no reporting back.

Sharing in pairs (**10 minutes**)

Companionship
(20 minutes)

The second reason in the service we will look at is what we might call companionship, or friendship. Most couples meet as friends first of all, before they fall in love. For some, that means that friendship gets pushed into second place. Being lovers is the task of the moment. But in the end, friendship is the longest-lasting of all these three. Sex will, I hope, still be important when you are 80; but it will be less important than now. If you have children, they will probably have left home by then. But you might be leaning on each other – literally as well as metaphorically. Being friends is a basic requirement for a good marriage. But what makes a good friend? Let's share some thoughts on that.

List elements of friendship on a flip chart or OHP, followed by general discussion. (**5 minutes**)

Many people include in their wedding service those famous words from Kahlil Gibran's *The Prophet*:

> *And stand together, yet not too near together,*
> *For the pillars of the temple stand apart*
> *And the oak tree and the cypress grow not in each other's shadow.*

There is great wisdom in that. How we spend time – together and apart; with friends as well as with each other – is something we all have to negotiate. Sometimes it can be quite surprising to work out just how much time we have together. On the piece of paper you have (*Resource sheet 7*), you will find four columns, headed 'Alone', 'Apart, but with others', 'Together' and 'Together with others', and a week's worth of days. Think through the last week, [since we were last together,] and roughly tot up how many of your waking hours fell into each of those four categories. It may not have been a typical week – but it was a real one! Work in pairs together in this room.

Work in pairs (**5 minutes**)

Do the figures surprise you? How do you feel about them? How do you negotiate your use of time? Is it easy or difficult to let the other one have time that could have been spent together meeting with friends, or pursuing individual activities? How do you keep a balance?

Read or retell the story of Bob and Miranda (Growing Together, *pp. 33–4*).

How do you feel about the way they handled things? Would it work for you?

General discussion (**5 minutes**)

Sex
(20 minutes)

That leaves us with sex. The *Common Worship* Preface is daring enough to use the word 'sexual'. I am glad about that. There has been a myth around for far too long that God and sex don't mix, and you shouldn't mention things like that in front of the vicar. As you may know, there are three sexes: men, women and clergy. Well, I have news for you: that is rubbish. You only have to take a step back to see what nonsense it is. If we believe that God made us, he made us as sexual beings, or at least allowed us to develop into sexual beings. We could still be splitting like amoeba, but it wouldn't be much fun. Sex is God's gift to us and, far from being naughty, it is something holy and wonderful and to be celebrated. But, like any other skill, although it is the most natural thing in the world, it has to be learned, and your task is to be each other's teachers. Men don't know a thing about being women, and women don't know a thing about being men, (although they sometimes like to pretend they do). However good any sex education we had was – and the chances are it wasn't all that good – we still have to learn a lot from each other, and to go on learning, because how we like to express love physically will change as the years go by.

Our attitudes may well be coloured by our upbringings. I wonder how much you have shared those with each other? It can raise issues. A person from a prudish kind of home may find living with a partner who comes from a home where nudity and openness about sex is normal quite a threat. I have to say it is surprisingly often the men who are more threatened than the women!

Read or retell the stories of Mike and Julie, and Kevin and Mandy (Growing Together, *p. 80*).

Many couples take quite a long time to settle down sexually. If that is the case for you, just be assured that is very normal. But if you are really having some problems, do look for help sooner rather than later. Why miss out on something that God intends to be so good?

I want you individually now to fill in this piece of paper (*Resource sheet 8*). It has two columns – 'Biggest turn-ons' and 'Biggest turn-offs' – and two sections – 'For me' and 'For you'. Take a couple of minutes now to write what you want on those (without looking at what your partner is writing!).

Individual work (**3 minutes**)

Now I *could* ask you to join in a general discussion about that – but one of the important things about sex is that it is intimate and private. So I am going to ask you to go with your own partner again, and just compare and share what you have written. Then can you move on to the more general question, which is at the foot of that sheet of paper: 'What does sex add to your whole relationship?'

Sharing in pairs (**12 minutes**)

Ending
(10 minutes)

(If timings have gone well, there should be about ten minutes left. If not, you will need to edit or omit all or part of this final section.)

As last week, you have a piece of paper provided (*Resource sheet 4*) with two columns. One has an exclamation mark on it, the other a question mark. Under the exclamation mark, would you jot down *individually* any new thought that has occurred to you this evening? It doesn't have to be something profound! And under the question mark put down anything that has raised questions you want to pursue further. There will be an opportunity at the beginning of next week, if you want it, to share anything that has come out of this evening – but no pressure to say anything if you prefer not to.

Individual responses (2 minutes)

We will stay together in this room, but now, in pairs, but with someone *other* than your partner, just take two minutes to share any 'exclamation mark' thoughts that have come to you as a result of this evening.

Sharing in pairs (2 minutes)

And then, with your *real* partner, share any 'question mark' areas which have come up this evening and which you would like to explore further with each other.

Sharing as couples (2 minutes)

It may be that this evening has raised some personal issues for you that you didn't want to share with the group, or even with each other. Do feel free to speak to me, if you want some time to talk anything through individually.

Lastly, let's take a minute or two in silence to reflect on all that has been said together, and privately. I will then offer all those thoughts to God in a short prayer to close.

Week 3: Communication

Introduction and non-verbal communication
(10 minutes)

Welcome back. I hope that if you had things you wanted to discuss further with each other, you have found time to do it. Does anyone want to comment on things they have discussed? There is *no obligation* to do so, but it would be good if you want to share a word or two about anything with each other.

Feedback **(3 minutes)**

One of the basic skills we all need is good communication. Certainly the most common thing people say when they go for marriage counselling is that communications have broken down. There are two parts to that, aren't there? One is talking – because if you don't talk to each other, how can you know what the other one thinks and feels? Silence can be wonderful, when it is relaxed companionable silence; we don't need to talk all the time, because it is nice just 'to be'. But when it is awkward and a sign of tension, it can also be awful. But the second skill is listening. If people don't listen, it doesn't matter how much someone talks. In these exercises we are about to do, we will all stay in this room, although we will be working in pairs, because I won't be asking you share anything private. I am going to get you to do some talking and listening in a moment. But just to remind you that words are not the only way of communicating, let's try one or two things. First, could you just take your intended's hand, and take it in turn to express an emotion by the way you hold it. Close your eyes for this one; otherwise you will also be using facial expressions, which is another important way of communicating.

Hand messages **(2 minutes)**

And since I asked you to close your eyes last time, let's now see how many emotions you can express to each other by way of facial expressions. Take it in turn, and check whether the message has been accurately received.

Facial expressions (2 minutes)

Speaking, hearing and listening
(25 minutes)

Now let's move on with a bit of listening and talking. We will do lots of exercises tonight, and my job will be to keep time for you. So don't worry about keeping an eye on your watch – I will ensure you get the messages about when to stop and what to do next.

First of all, find someone other than your partner. Just talk to them for a minute – non-stop – about what you did yesterday. Both of you do it *at the same time* – just talk *at* each other, without listening to the other. It's up to you to keep going.

Simultaneous talk (1 minute)

How did that feel? (2 minutes)

Now work with your proper partner. Would one person in each couple first of all tell a story – perhaps about something that happened to you when the other person wasn't there. You have just two minutes. Meanwhile, would the other person please do their very best to ignore him or her. Look the other way; fiddle with your watch; whatever you like – but don't pay any attention.

Ignored talk (2 minutes)

Now reverse roles, and do that again.

Ignored talk (2 minutes)

What did that feel like?

General discussion (2 minutes)

Now let's have another story, this time from the distant past. Maybe you could talk about your first day at your secondary school, or the day you left school. But it can be a story about anything. You have two minutes to tell it. This time the listener should pay full attention, because you will be asked to recall what you heard.

Careful listening (2 minutes)

Could the listener please now recount that story. You have one minute.

Recall (1 minute)

As before, can you now reverse roles, so the storyteller becomes the listener. Again you have two minutes for the story, and then a minute to recount what you heard.

Careful listening (2 minutes)

Could the listener now recount that story? You have one minute.

Recall (1 minute)

Let's now talk together about what doing that felt like.

(*You may want to use some of these prompts*: Was it easier to be the talker or the listener? What things make listening difficult? What helped you to talk? What did it feel like when you heard your story being accurately / inaccurately retold? Did the things that were missed out matter?)

General discussion (**5 minutes**)

Now let's take that one stage further. I hope you can still remember those two stories you each told. What I would like you to do now, in your pairs, is to try to recall not the *facts* of those stories, but the *emotions* that were being carried by them. What did you think the person talking was *feeling*? You have just a minute each to try to do that.

Recall of feelings (**2 minutes**)

How easy is it to pick up another person's emotions? How easy do you find it to express them?

General discussion (**3 minutes**)

Other ways of communicating
(15 minutes)

We're going to do some more work on this in pairs in a moment, but while we are still all together, let's just think about any other ways we use to communicate, apart from the things we have already looked at (touch; facial expressions; speech).

(Hopefully the group will come up with other things – but if they don't, prompt with things like: body language, clothes, smell (pheromones as well as perfumes – it is something we do naturally), music, lighting, tears, laughter . . .)

General discussion (**15 minutes**)

Improving our skills
(30 minutes)

Most people love to be understood and hate it when they are *mis*understood. We relish having someone's undivided attention, because it affirms that we matter and that what we think and say matters. The Children's Society once ran a very perceptive campaign with the slogan 'This child needs a good listening to'. So do we all.

I am going to ask you to go off in your pairs for half an hour now. How you use that time is up to you. You have 15 minutes each (and we will make a suitable noise to let you all know when we reach half-time). I am not so much concerned about *what* you talk about as the *way* you talk about it. Can I suggest you each pick an issue that concerns you, excites you, puzzles you – *but nothing too major*, because there isn't time to deal with something like that. Talk about it for a while – certainly no more than ten minutes – using all those skills of attentive listening and playing back and reading body language and facial expression, tone of voice, and all the other things we have mentioned. Then take a step back and see how it felt: what helped, and what hindered good communication. Then, when half-time comes, the other one has the chance to raise *their* issue, and you deal with it in the same way. Remember, we can all improve our listening, understanding and talking skills. No one is perfect at it!

Work in pairs (**30 minutes**)

Ending
(10 minutes)

As last week, you have a piece of paper provided (*Resource sheet 4*) with two columns. One has an exclamation mark on it, the other a question mark. Under the exclamation mark, would you jot down *individually* any new thought that has occurred to you this evening. It doesn't have to be anything profound! And under the question mark put down anything that has raised questions you want to pursue further. There will be an opportunity at the beginning of next week, if you want it, to share anything that has come out of this evening – but there will be no pressure to say anything if you prefer not to.

Individual responses (**2 minutes**)

We will stay together in this room, but now, in pairs, but with someone *other* than your partner, just take two minutes to share any 'exclamation mark' thoughts that have come to you as a result of this evening.

Sharing in pairs (**2 minutes**)

And then, with your *real* partner, share any 'question mark' areas which have come up this evening and which you would like to explore further with each other.

Sharing as couples (**2 minutes**)

It may be that this evening has raised some personal issues for you that you didn't want to share with the group, or even with each other. Do feel free to speak to me if you want some time to talk anything through individually.

Lastly, let's take a minute or two in silence to reflect on all that has been said, both together and privately. I will then offer all those thoughts to God in a short prayer to close.

Week 4: Conflict

Introduction
(5 minutes)

Welcome back. I hope that, if you had things you wanted to discuss further with each other, you have found time to do it. Does anyone want to comment on things they have discussed? You don't have to; but if you do want to share a word or two about anything with the group, that would be good.

Feedback (**3 minutes**)

In this session we are going to spend time looking at how we handle conflict. That isn't being negative; it is facing up to the fact that being married is not always easy. That doesn't reflect on the reality of your love. It reflects the fact that a marriage is two individuals trying to work as a team.

Being realistic
(20 minutes)

You have a piece of paper (*Resource sheet 11*), which has two columns, and there are lots of blank lines for you to fill in. In your pairs I want you as quickly as you can to fill in as many lines as you can. Each of you has a column, so put your name at the top of it. What I would like you to do is think of as many ways as you can in which you are different from each other. The paper gives you a start with the most obvious: one is male, the other female. People sometimes say 'We have our differences', meaning that they disagree. But differences are not necessarily a problem – in fact, they can be very positive. If one of you wasn't male and the other female, you wouldn't be here tonight! So when you have filled in as many as you want, then will you circle the ones which are a plus factor for you – differences that are a good thing – and put a square round the ones which are a problem, or a potential problem for you – differences that are a bad thing. And there will probably be several that are neither one thing nor the other; and maybe some that are both!

Work in pairs (**10 minutes**)

You have another piece of paper with four rough graphs (*Resource sheet 3*). The first three are unrealistic maps of how a marriage will be. The first represents ever-increasing bliss. The second represents ever-increasing misery. The third represents no change at all – everything just as it is, for ever. If you think that any of those is how your relationships are, then you have a problem.

The last one is the reality. There will be ups and downs in everyone's relationships; the vital thing is how we handle them.

What I would like you to have a go at is plotting individually, on the back of that sheet, a graph of how you as an individual see your relationship so far – hopefully there haven't been major downs, but there will almost certainly have been little blips – maybe stresses caused from outside, when a house you hoped to buy fell through, or when there was a bereavement.

Graph plotting (**3 minutes**)

Now go with your partner and compare notes; talk about what you have drawn, and whether you see the ups and down in the same way.

Sharing in pairs (**5 minutes**)

Recognizing our skills
(**10 minutes**)

The chapter about 'Conflict' in *Growing Together* uses the analogy of a first-aid box. Having one in the house is very sensible – but it is important to know where it is, and what is in it. Then when a crisis comes and you have cut your finger, you know where you can get help. The vast majority of the conflicts we have in relationships are going to be solved by our relationship first-aid box – that collection of bits and pieces that we have acquired which we know can help. Let's first of all share the kind of things that might be in it. What are the everyday ways in which we can get over glitches in our relationships? What helps us to make up and move on?

(*With the group's help, list a few possibilities on a flip chart or OHP.*)

Those are a few things in general. What is important are the things you have in your personal first-aid box. In pairs, can you go off and make your own personal list of the things that help you get through bad moments. If you are willing to share some of them when we come together again, that would be useful.

Work in pairs (**5 minutes**)

Sharing ideas (add to list on a flip chart or OHP) (**3 minutes**)

Outside help
(**10 minutes**)

Sometimes a first-aid box doesn't have the right things in it. You need a prescription from the doctor for your upset tummy, or whatever. Your GP is the next line of defence you have, medically; what are the equivalents in terms of relationship ills? Family and friends. Let's put on a list the pluses and minuses of using them to help if things are difficult.

List on a flip chart or OHP (**5 minutes**)

It is all going to depend on what your family and friends are like and what the nature of the problem is – and indeed, *when* the problem occurs. You might normally feel that you could talk to Mum or Dad – but not just now, because they are going on holiday tomorrow, and you don't want them to be worried while they are away.

If your medical problem really *is* a crisis, then you forget the first-aid box and the GP and go off to the nearest A&E Department. I wonder if we can list what the equivalent places may be for a crisis in a relationship?

List on a flip chart or OHP (*prompting if necessary: clergy, counsellor, financial adviser, doctor, etc.*) (**5 minutes**)

Facing difficult facts
(**10 minutes**)

Marriages can be dangerous things. The present statistics show that one in every three women will suffer domestic violence at some point in their lives – how many statistically are there in this room, therefore? What is more, the average victim does not go to the police until there have been 33 occasions of violence. So maybe the figures are even more shocking than we realize. And it is not just women who are victims. The figures for men are that one in every seven suffer domestic violence. Men are also much less likely to report such happenings. Once violence has happened – or nearly happened – it changes the way people think of each other. The Bible talks about perfect love casting out fear, but unfortunately the reverse is also true. Fear can cast out love, and violence breeds fear.

In your pairs, I would like you to talk about these statistics, and what they make you feel. It is all about anger; so, when you have talked about the issue in general, can you discuss how each of you handles anger – something that we all have, and which may be justified. But although anger can be justifiable, violence never can.

Work in pairs (**10 minutes**)

What would you do?
(**25 minutes**)

On this sheet of paper (*Resource sheet 12*) you have four situations. You won't have time to look at all of them in this session; but there is always the chance to look at the others at home. The questions are the same for each one:

1 What is the obvious problem?
2 Are there other problems that might lie behind it?
3 Do you think the couple concerned should be able to solve it for themselves?
- If so, what can *each* of them do to contribute to the solution?
- If not, what sort of outside help might they look for?

Ending
(10 minutes)

As last week, you have a piece of paper provided (*Resource sheet 4*) with two columns. One has an exclamation mark on it, the other a question mark. Under the exclamation mark would you jot down *individually* any new thought that has occurred to you this evening. It doesn't have to be anything profound! And under the question mark put down anything that has raised questions you want to pursue further. There will be an opportunity at the beginning of next week, if you want it, to share anything that has come out of this evening – but no pressure to say anything if you prefer not to.

Individual responses (2 minutes)

We will stay together in this room, but now, in pairs, but with someone *other* than your partner, just take two minutes to share any 'exclamation mark' thoughts that have come to you as a result of this evening.

Sharing in pairs (2 minutes)

And then, with your *real* partner, share any 'question mark' areas which have come up this evening and which you would like to explore further with each other.

Sharing as couples (2 minutes)

It may be that this evening has raised some personal issues for you that you didn't want to share with the group, or even with each other. Do feel free to speak to me if you want some time to talk anything through individually.

Lastly, let's take a minute or two in silence to reflect on all that has been said together, and privately. I will then offer all those thoughts to God in a short prayer to close.

Week 5: Spiritual issues

Introduction
(3 minutes)

Welcome back. I hope that, if you had things you wanted to discuss further with each other, you have found time to do it. Does anyone want to comment on things they have discussed? You don't have to, but if you do want to share a word or two about anything with the group, that would be good.

Feedback (3 minutes)

Beliefs
(10 minutes)

A long time ago people used to talk about marriage as 'getting spliced'. It's a phrase that has gone out of use, but it is really rather a good one. We are made up, so Christians say, of three parts: body, mind and soul. Usually bodies and minds get spliced all right, but often the soul bit is not so well joined. It is ways into thinking of that which concern us this time; but you may be surprised at how wide that might take us.

But let's start with obviously religious issues. I could ask you all to tell me your partner's religious beliefs, but you might be relieved to know that I'm not going to. What I *will* ask is for you to show whether you could confidently have done so if I had asked you. I want you to imagine a line running diagonally from this corner of the room to that one (*indicate corners as you speak*). If you are totally confident that you know your partner's beliefs, you need to be right in that corner (*indicate*). If you are totally confident that you haven't the faintest idea what they are, you need to be in the opposite corner. But I guess most of you will want to place yourself somewhere along the imaginary line between the two. Let's go to the appropriate place now.

(*Participants place themselves on imaginary line.*)

As we stand in those places, let's think for a moment *why* we are where we are. What are the things that make us confident or otherwise? If we are in the middle, *why* are we not very sure?

General discussion

The reasons are probably very obvious: if you have talked a lot about it, then you will be sure, and if it is a fairly closed book, then you won't be. There are very respectable reasons for it being a closed book. You might not be very good at putting your beliefs into words. You might be afraid of being laughed at, or of having something you feel strongly about challenged. So the safe way is to say as little as possible. But one of the important things about the marriage relationship is *intimacy* – in other words, not having 'no go areas'.

Faith matters
(15 minutes)

There is one issue that you will all have talked about, or you would not be here – and that is the decision about whether you were going to get married in church. I am going to ask you all to write on a piece of paper *your* reason for getting married in church: not you as a couple; not your partner's reason; but *your own*. I am going to mix them up before I read them out, so there is no way people will know who said what, so please be ruthlessly honest. If your reason is to keep your parents quiet, or whatever, then say so.

Individual work; then shared (on a flip chart or OHP, if desired) **(5 minutes)**

Sometimes people think it is strange, or even wrong, that people who don't usually go to church want to have their wedding there. Imagine you are being interviewed for a TV programme by someone who thinks like that. What are the things you would want to say in reply? When you are interviewed in real life, there isn't much time to think – but you will have plenty of time to decide together the kind of things you would include in your response. You might like to jot down some bullet-points, but be assured, it is a private document, and you won't have to share it.

One of the rights you have in the *Common Worship* service is to write your own prayers for your wedding. Imagine the vicar has invited you to write a prayer which will be true to where you stand in matters of faith. There is a famous prayer which went 'O God, if there is a God, help me to save my soul, if I have a soul.' Again, your prayer is a private one, and not for publication.

Work in pairs **(15 minutes)**

There are lots of other religious issues that you will need to talk about from time to time. If you have children, will they be baptized? There may be quite a lot to talk about if you come from two different Christian traditions, or from two different faith backgrounds. You all come with an individual faith journey. It may be a long one, or a very short one. People often say, 'I'm not very religious.' Well, we are all believers or not believers. In others words, we all have a religious position that we are in at this moment. That may change; and changes like that can be a challenge in a marriage, if suddenly someone who has not been very religious gets religion big-time, or, for that matter, if someone who has been very religious loses their faith. Our faith journeys are personal, but they have an effect on each other.

Priorities and money
(25 minutes)

What are the most important things to you? You are going to do an exercise that will show up what is true for you. But I think we need to have a practice go at it together. You each have a sheet (*Resource sheet 14*). Here is one on the flip chart (*or OHP, if you are using that*). First of all, you compare row 1 with row 2. Put a mark against the one that is the more important. Now compare row 1 with row 3, and put a mark in that same column against the more important one. Do that all the way down, comparing row 1 with each of the others. Now take row 2 (forget the row above) and do the same, comparing it with rows 3, 4 and so on, and mark those in the second thin column. Then take row 3 and compare it with all the rows below in the third column. Do that all the way through, and then add up the number of marks in each row. The subject with the highest number of marks is your first priority. Is everyone clear what they have to do? I have put seven items in. You might want to add one or two more for yourself.

So would you go off and do that, first of all individually. Then compare notes with your partner, to see if your priorities are the same. If you add your individual results for each row together, then you will get your joint order of priorities. Are they the same as your individual ones? Or different? Take ten minutes to do that, and then we'll talk about it.

Work in pairs (10 minutes)

Let's now take another issue which is very spiritual, and which might help you think about the deepest issues – and that is money. How we spend our money – or at least the part of it left when the mortgage/rent/council tax/utility bills have been paid – reveals the things that are most important to us. And our attitudes to money can often be rooted in our childhood.

Read or retell the story of Michael and Judith (Growing Together, *pp. 66–7*).

It might be quite interesting for you to look at your priority list and see how it compares with how you spend your money. They won't match, because something that is a high priority might demand very little cash, and something much lower down the list might be quite expensive, but nonetheless, it is something you might like to do at home.

What I would like you to do now, in pairs, is to talk about how you make financial decisions and how you handle your money. Do you have a joint account? Two separate accounts? Three accounts? Or do you keep your money under the bed? How do you budget (unless you are one of the tiny minority who don't need to!)? In particular, do you budget to give money away? People are very generous in responding to things like *Children in Need* – but that is when somebody jogs your elbow. What is even better is when couples decide in advance what they can afford to give to people who need help, and make sure their giving is tax efficient by Gift-Aiding it. Are there things you both care about enough to put them into your regular budget? You may not be able to afford much at the moment, but the principle of giving being a priority is worth talking about. You have these financial questions on a sheet (*Resource sheet 13*) – go and spend ten minutes looking at some of them now, and look at the rest at home if you don't finish. These are spiritual issues as well as practical ones.

Work in pairs (**10 minutes**)

Questions of life and death
(**25 minutes**)

Alan Bennett wrote a sketch about a woman who had her dead husband's ashes made into an egg-timer. Her philosophy was that he had never done anything useful in his life, and it would be satisfying to think that he was useful after he had gone. Talking about death is never easy, but the wedding service doesn't shrink from it ('till death do us part . . .'), so neither should we. Just for a moment, think about what you would like put on your tombstone. You may know the story of the Yorkshire mason who was asked to inscribe one stone with the words 'He was thine', but missed off the last letter, so that it read 'He was thin'. The family rang him up and complained he had left the 'e' off. He apologized; and in due course the stone came back reading 'Ee, he was thin'. Just a minute to decide your epitaph and then let's go round and share them.

(*Individual work, and then shared*)

More seriously, let's think about the implications of 'till death do us part'. Hopefully that will be many years hence for all of you – but it has to happen one day. It is very good practice to make a will after your wedding. If you already have one, getting married means you need to do it again. I am going to ask you to talk about that in your pairs in a moment or two. Unless someone pushes you into talking about death, you won't do it. People don't come home and say, 'Let's talk about death tonight' – not usually, anyway! But also I want you to talk about one or two aspects of dying that need a decision in advance. The first is whether you want to be buried or cremated. The second is whether you want to donate some or all of your body for transplants or medical research. At the moment we have to opt into organ donation, and there is a great need for people to do so. It is a decision to be made not in the crisis of a death, but now. There are no rights and wrongs. It is a very personal matter, and one that is worth discussing. It can go in your will, as well as being registered online. All this talk about death is useful much earlier in your marriage than 'till death do us part' implies. You will have to support each other through other family bereavements long before then, and you will be best equipped to help each other if death has not been a taboo subject. So take 15 minutes to talk through how you both feel about these issues and to share your experiences of bereavement, from the death of childhood pets onwards. How do you cope with these eternal questions of life and death?

Work in pairs (**10 minutes**)

Ending
(**10 minutes**)

As last week, you have a piece of paper provided (*Resource sheet 4*) with two columns. One has an exclamation mark on it, the other a question mark. Under the exclamation mark would you jot down *individually* any new thought that has occurred to you this evening. It doesn't have to be something profound! And under the question mark put down anything that has raised questions you want to pursue further. There will be an opportunity at the beginning of next week, if you want it, to share anything that has come out of this evening – but no pressure to say anything if you prefer not to.

Individual responses (2 minutes)

We will stay together in this room, but now in pairs, but with someone *other* than your partner; just take two minutes to share any 'exclamation mark' thoughts that have come to you as a result of this evening.

Sharing in pairs (2 minutes)

And then, with your *real* partner, share any 'question mark' areas which have come up this evening and which you would like to explore further with each other.

Sharing as couples (2 minutes)

It may be that this evening has raised some personal issues for you that you didn't want to share with the group, or even with each other. Do feel free to speak to me if you want some time to talk anything through individually.

Lastly, let's take a minute or two in silence to reflect on all that has been said, both together and privately. I will then offer all those thoughts to God in a short prayer to close.

Week 6: Us and them

Introduction
(5 minutes)

Welcome back. I hope that if you had things you wanted to discuss further with each other, you have found time to do it. Does anyone want to comment on things they have discussed? There is no obligation to do so, but if you want to share a word or two about anything with each other, that would be good.

Feedback (3 minutes)

Who does what?
(20 minutes)

Read or retell the story of Colin and Bernice (Growing Together, *pp. 74–5*).

On Resource sheet 15 we have a number of household tasks, and some blank spaces as well. Let's just brainstorm some other things that *someone* has to do in every home, and you can fill them in on your sheets.

Brainstorm ideas

Now would you work in pairs – we'll stay together in this room to do this one. Fill in on your sheet who *used* to do each task in your home when you were a child. Then put who does them in *your* home; or who you will expect to do it, if you are not living together already. Then compare notes, and talk about whether the work is divided in a way that you are both comfortable about. When we come back together we'll just list the things that caused the most arguments!

Work in pairs (**5 minutes**)

Reporting back (**5 minutes**)

Those are the practical things. But there will be some more general things where you have different roles: things like being a spender or a saver; or being a decision maker, or finding it hard to decide on things. I hope your individual strengths and weaknesses balance each other out to some extent. Spend ten minutes deciding in what ways that is true for you.

Work in pairs (**10 minutes**)

The wider family
(**20 minutes**)

Getting married joins together two families as well as two individuals. But every family is different, and affects how that happens.

Read or retell the stories of Greg and Jo, and Kevin and Maggie (Growing Together, *pp. 58– 9*).

For the next 15 minutes, go and draw a family map. (*Flip chart paper would be useful for this.*) It doesn't matter how you draw it, as long as you both understand what it means. The example sheet you have (*Resource sheet 16*) is just using some of the conventional symbols to guide you. You might want to place people nearer to you or further away from you, according to how much you see them; or to put brackets round them if you aren't in touch with them at all.

When you have drawn your map, with however many people you want to include, have a look at it and see what similarities and what differences there are between your two families of origin. Do those similarities and differences affect the way you both think about the wider family?

Work in pairs (**15 minutes**)

The place we live in
(**20 minutes**)

The *Common Worship* wedding service talks about the effects of marriage being wider even than your families: 'It enriches society and strengthens community.'

Let's spend a few minutes sharing ideas about how you think that can happen. (*If they are not mentioned, add ideas about how happy homes make for happier places of work, better health, etc. It is even true that some of the current need to build more houses is partly because of the numbers of people living alone through the failure of relationships – and that affects the environment for everyone.*)

Brainstorm (**10 minutes**)

Last of all, in pairs, share together what very specific things you think you can give to your community life at the moment. The amount of time and energy people have will change as work and family demands change, so it is very much a question of what is possible *now*. Do either of you do anything to help community life, through voluntary groups, etc? Is that something one or both of you might consider? It is part of your marriage whether or not you are both involved – if one of you goes to do something, the other must be happy to let them go!

Work in pairs (**10 minutes**)

Ending
(25 minutes)

As in previous weeks, you have a piece of paper provided (*Resource sheet 4*) with two columns. One has an exclamation mark on it, the other a question mark. Under the exclamation mark, would you jot down *individually* any new thought that has occurred to you this evening. It doesn't have to be something profound! And under the question mark put down anything that has raised questions you want to pursue further. This week, we will just share our 'question mark' areas and 'exclamation mark' areas with our *real* partners.

Individual responses (2 minutes)

Sharing in pairs (3 minutes)

But this week we have another, similar sheet. Because next week is a very different session, when we will be looking at the wedding day itself and the choices and decisions you have to make about it, this is really the last chance we will have for any general questions or comments you want to make about the last six sessions we have spent together. As couples, just jot down the things which are the 'question marks' and 'exclamation marks' that have come out of the *whole of the course*, and then we will briefly share whatever we want to about how we feel as we end it.

Work in pairs (5 minutes)

General discussion (15 minutes)

It may be that this evening, or the course as a whole, has raised some personal issues for you that you didn't want to share with the group, or even with each other. Do feel free to speak to me if you want some time to talk anything through individually.

Lastly, let's take a minute or two in silence to reflect on all that has been said together, and privately. I will then offer all those thoughts to God in a short prayer to close.

Week 7: The wedding day

(How this is organized, and the timings, will depend on your local situation. You may want this session to be in church, so that the organist can play and the flower arrangers can show where the flowers can be placed, and so on. The suggestions below are the agenda items that can usefully be included.)

This will be your day – and they are your choices. Personalize as much as you can. You may want to involve other people in what happens. You will need to check everything through with the vicar.

Order of service

Strictly speaking, there are three orders of service that are legal: the 1662 Book of Common Prayer, the 1928 Prayer Book (Series 1) and *Common Worship* (2000). In practice, *Common Worship* probably has everything you might want, including a form of wedding with Holy Communion, which is an option any of you who are regular communicants might want to consider. It doesn't have to add a lot of time to the service.

Choreography

- Who walks in with whom
- Where people stand or sit
- 'Giving away' or alternatives
- Where you sign the registers
- Other practical issues

Hymns

- There is space in service for four, but you don't have to have that many.
- The most important thing is that people should know the hymns chosen. It's embarrassing for the vicar to have to sing a solo!
- Some fit in one place better than another. So, for example, a hymn about vows goes well at the point when you are about to make them, or a hymn which is a prayer just before the prayers. It's also generally best to go out on the most joyous note.
- Check that the tune the organist has in mind is also the tune you are expecting. Some popular hymns, such as 'Love divine' or 'At the name of Jesus', have more than one well-known tune.
- Copyright issues.
- Start thinking now! People often pick up ideas when they go to church on Sundays, or to other people's weddings.

Readings

- Who? This is a good opportunity to involve other people, but readers do need to practise, especially if the reading(s) chosen contain tricky names (such as Balaam).
- What? At least one of the readings must come from the Bible. There are 26 suggestions in *Common Worship* (but you can choose others if you wish).
- Take care to read them all; then cut them down to a short list. Why do the readings on your short list speak to you?
- Let me share with you two readings that, after the 1 Corinthians reading, I find are being chosen very often these days. The first is from the Song of Solomon (sometimes called 'the Song of Songs'). It is a really quite erotic poem, which talks about God's love in terms of human passion. The reading doesn't include the parts about the beloved's breasts being like twin fawns, or clusters of grapes, or the man's legs being like alabaster columns set upon bases of gold. This is the bit that it does use. You need to think of a woman hiding behind the lattice window of a Middle Eastern house, with the lover whispering through the window. (Incidentally, it says in another place that he has arrived there bounding like a young gazelle across the desert.) This is how it goes.
- [Read Song of Solomon 2.10-13; 8.6-7.]
- The second is from the Apocrypha – the books from Old Testament times that were left out of some versions of the Bible. This one is from the book of Tobit.
- [Read Tobit 8.4-8.]

- The context of that one is rather fun too, but you wouldn't guess it from the bit we heard. The couple are praying before their first night together. But Sarah has been previously given in marriage to seven other men. Unfortunately, before the marriage could be consummated, they were all killed by a demon called Asmodeus. Now, people were as sceptical then about the reality of demons as they are now, and they quite reasonably said it was Sarah who killed them off. Now, if you think this story is bizarre, I have to say 'You ain't heard nothin' yet!' Tobias is very smitten with Sarah, but he has a meeting with the Archangel Raphael, and after another curious incident when a huge fish tries to swallow Tobias's foot when he washes it in the Tigris, he is told by the angel to catch the fish and eat the flesh, but to keep the gall, heart and liver, because they are useful in dealing with demons. So, come his first night with Sarah, when they are obviously both on edge that he might become Victim Number Eight, he takes the precaution of burning these bits of old fish guts as a way of dealing with Asmodeus – which works. Apparently it smells so bad he takes off to Upper Egypt, where Raphael deals with him once and for all.
- Make sure you have the translation you want – and that the reader knows which one will be on the lectern at the service.
- Non-biblical readings are very personal and entirely optional. The most important point is that what you choose means something to you. All such readings need to be OK'd with the vicar. Some brave brides and grooms have written something themselves.

Prayers

- Yet again, this is an opportunity to make the service very much your own.
- One set of prayers is printed in the main text of the service, but there are many others to choose from in *Common Worship: Pastoral Services*. The idea generally is that you choose *either* one of the longer ones (with the 'response' style) *or* one from each of the sections of short prayers.
- Prayers can also be chosen from elsewhere.
- Or you can write your own!

Music

Music sets the tone for the service and is an important part of it. There are three basic places where it is used:

- Entry
- Registers – probably 5–7 minutes' worth
- Exit.

The organ is the usual instrument, but do make sure the music you choose will suit both the building and the organ. People can be led astray by listening to discs. Do also make sure that the organist can play what you choose.

If you want to use a recording of music at any of these points in the service, do check that a system is available to play it on. It may be worth your while to burn the exact track to a CD, rather than risking that the wrong track may be played!

Consider also whether live music – from friends or family – may be a possibility for you.

Oddments

- Banns
- Fees
- Confetti
- Photos and/or videos
- Other practical issues.

Ending

- Thank you for coming to this course. I hope that it has been useful to you.
- Do any of you have any further questions you would like to ask? (*Deal with any questions posed by members of the group.*)
- Give out copies of *Growing Together*.
- Explain to group what to do about any further queries they may have (*e.g. individual queries by phone etc.*).
- Arrangements for rehearsals.
- Pray the prayer below, to end the last session.

> *There are so many choices:*
> > *venues and menus,*
> > *dresses and tresses,*
> > *shades and bridesmaids,*
> > *cars and guitars,*
> > *houses and blouses,*
> > *speeches and preachers;*
> *It is so easy to over-spend, to lose all sense of proportion.*
> *Help us to plan not only for the day, but for the rest of our life.*
> *Help us to choose the best things:*
> > *faith*
> > *hope*
> > *love.*

(Andrew Body, from *Pocket Prayers for Marriage*)

Scripted version for 'How have we grown? A reunion course'

Introduction

(10–15 minutes)

Each couple should be asked in advance to bring with them a picture, or an object, that reminds them of their wedding or honeymoon.

Most of you have been married between nine months and a year now. Let's reintroduce ourselves.

(Go round the group. Each couple should give the following information.)

- Names
- When married
- Comment on photo or object.

Things move on

(25 minutes)

Now let's share two of the most important things that have happened to each couple in the time you have been married.

Group discussion **(10 minutes)**

Those are things that have happened *to* you. Now we are going to have some time in private to identify three things for each of you. These are private discussions; there will be no reporting back.

- Something that has been a surprise – why was that?
- Something that has been better than you expected – why was that?
- Something that has been a disappointment – why was that?

Work in pairs **(15 minutes)**

How are the reasons for marriage developing?

(30 minutes)

The wedding service identified three reasons for getting married: companionship and friendship, sex, and children.

In your pairs, take stock now of how those three things have changed and developed. How are things different between you from before you were married? Why have they changed? Are those changes all good? If not, what can you do about it?

You have half an hour, so divide the time between the three categories as you choose.

Work in pairs **(30 minutes)**

Current dreams

(10 minutes)

Alexander Solzhenitsyn said that marriage was like riding a bicycle. You have to keep moving forward, or you wobble and fall off. So we need to go on having dreams and making them come true if we can. What are your dreams for the next year? Are there any ways in which the members of this group could go on supporting one another? Would you like to meet again?

Group discussion (**10 minutes**)

Saying 'Thank you'

(10 minutes)

Use a simple form of the service of Thanksgiving for Marriage printed in *Common Worship: Pastoral Services*. It can be found on Resource sheet 18 and on the CD-ROM.

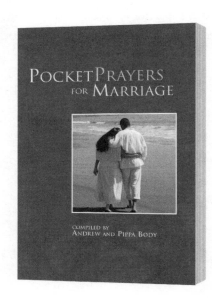